Sharon James reveals how heartfelt communion with God was not merely a duty but a delight for Jonathan Edwards' wife, Sarah. Reading Sarah Edwards' first-hand account of how God met with her in an extraordinary way will encourage the reader to pray for and work toward revival today.

Karin Stetina, Associate Professor of Biblical and Theological Studies, Biola University and author of *Jonathan Edwards' Early Understanding of Religious Experience*

Sharon James's portrait of Sarah Edwards is a deeply moving case study in what Jesus meant when he said, 'For where your treasure is, there your heart will be also' (Matthew 6:21). Sarah Edwards' delight in God will increase your desire to experience what Scripture so wonderfully promises: 'Delight yourself in the Lord, and he will give you the desires of your heart' (Psalm 37:4).

Jon Bloom, author & cofounder of Desiring God

On the work of the Holy Spirit in Christian experience, Sarah Edwards' testimony from 1742 has a place of enduring significance. Sharon James uses Sarah's own account as a centre-piece in this attractive and challenging biography. *Sarah Edwards: Delighting in God* will introduce many new readers to a period of evangelical history important for today.

Iain H. Murray, speaker & author of numerous books including *Jonathan Edwards: A New Biography*

Sharon James's delightful account brings a remarkable eighteenth-century woman of deep spirituality to life. This is a vibrant, heart-warming, historical account which challenges us for biblical twenty-first-century living. Sarah Edwards' deep sense of sin, experience of the overwhelming love of God and her joy in her Saviour will bring you closer to the Lord Jesus as you similarly trust in his sovereign care. This is an inspiring book.

Elinor Magowan, Director for Women's Ministry, FIEC

I've been hoping for another biography by Sharon James, and *Sarah Edwards Delighting in God* does not disappoint. Sarah Edwards didn't lead an easy life but her extraordinary experience of the love of God left her longing to know ever deeper the God in whom she delighted. Read *Sarah Edwards* and find yourself caught up in the love of God alongside her, and then pray for revival in your own heart, church and city.

Keri Folmar, speaker & author

Sarah Edwards
Delighting in God

EP

Sarah Edwards
Delighting in God

SHARON JAMES

'The glory of God seemed to be all,
and in all, and to swallow up every
wish and desire of my heart … my
soul was filled and overwhelmed with
light, and love, and joy.'

British Cataloguing in Publication Data
A record for this book is available from the British Library

ISBN: 978-1-78397-339-2

Designed by Jude May
Cover image © Im-kseniabond | iStock

Printed in Denmark

Evangelical Press, an imprint of 10Publishing
Unit C, Tomlinson Road, Leyland, PR25 2DY, England
epbooks@10ofthose.com
www.epbooks.org

1 3 5 7 10 8 6 4 2

God is my great desire,
his face I seek the first;
to him my heart and soul aspire,
for him I thirst.
As one in desert lands,
whose very flesh is flame,
in burning love I lift my hands
and bless his name.

God is my true delight,
my richest feast his praise,
through silent watches of the night,
through all my days.
To him my spirit clings,
on him my soul is cast;
beneath the shadow of his wings
he holds me fast.

God is my strong defence
in every evil hour;
in him I face with confidence
the tempter's power.
I trust his mercy sure,
with truth and triumph crowned:
My hope and joy for evermore
In him are found.

Timothy Dudley-Smith[1]

Contents

Introduction

God's work wonderfully broke forth among us, and
souls began to flock to Christ as the Saviour in whose
righteousness alone they hoped to be justified.[1]

That is how Jonathan Edwards (1703–58) described the remarkable progress of the gospel in Northampton, New England, in 1734. Many were overjoyed at what they regarded as a glorious work of God. Others were horrified, regarding it all as dangerous fanaticism. When Edwards later set out to analyse the true and the false in revival, his own wife's experience provided him with a remarkable case study of the genuine work of the Spirit. Sarah (1710–58) provided him with a lived-out illustration of the reality of God's love.

Jonathan and Sarah Edwards lived in Massachusetts, one of the New England colonies. Jonathan is remembered as a leader in the First Great Awakening, and as a great theologian and philosopher. In the past he has been unfairly characterised as a harsh preacher, whose best-known sermon was 'Sinners in the Hands of an Angry God'. In the present, for some, the fact that he owned slaves negates the value of his legacy.[2] But we should not so quickly dismiss his ministry. Indeed, the central theme was the beauty, the glory and the love of God.

When I was a young teenager, I picked up a small booklet at a conference bookstall entitled *Heaven: A World of Love*.[3] At thirteen pence, it was within my budget. I bought it, read it and was gripped by the power and energy of the description of the beauty of God. That was my first encounter with Jonathan Edwards. From that time on, I knew that our greatest joy is to be found in God.

Nearly 20 years ago, I wrote a book entitled *In Trouble and In Joy*, which looked at the lives of four women, including Sarah Edwards. I have often returned to her detailed description of the three weeks in 1742 when God met with her in an extraordinary way. As well as an account of her life, this book includes, in full, her first-hand account of what happened during those three weeks (chapter 6).[4]

This is not merely of historic interest. God doesn't change. Sarah's testimony encourages us today to pray, and work, for revival, personal and communal.

Blessed be his glorious name forever,
May the whole earth be filled with his glory.
(Psalm 72:19)

Sharon James
London, 2022

New England, 1700

Timeline

1703	Jonathan Edwards born
1704	Deerfield massacre
1710	Sarah Pierpont born
1726	Sarah (age 16) 'was led to prize nearness to Christ as the creature's greatest happiness'
1727	February: Jonathan ordained as minister of religion at Northampton
1727	July: marriage of Jonathan (age 25) and Sarah (age 17)
1734–42	Revival at Northampton
1742	19 January–11 February: Sarah's intense experience of the love of God
1744	War between England and France, hostilities in North America
1750	Dismissal of Jonathan from the Northampton church
1751	Move to missionary settlement at Stockbridge
1758	Deaths of Jonathan (age 55) and Sarah (age 48)

PART 1

Desiring God

O God, you are my God;
earnestly I seek you;
my soul thirsts for you;
my flesh faints for you,
as in a dry and weary land
where there is no water.

Psalm 63:1

1

The setting

The Pilgrim Fathers disembarked from the *Mayflower* at Cape Cod in November 1620, the first of many thousands of English Puritans to settle around Massachusetts Bay. These were people who had left family and friends behind them, and travelled at risk of their lives into the unknown. For them, worshipping God was the most important thing in life. God should be worshipped in the way he has laid down in Scripture, and they refused to be forced into what they regarded as false worship. In his classic account, *Of Plymouth Plantation*, William Bradford described their situation:

> *When by the zeal of some godly preachers, and God's blessing on their labours, many in the North of England and other parts became enlightened by the word of God*

and had their ignorance and sins discovered to them, and began by His grace to reform their lives and pay heed to their ways, the work of God was no sooner manifest in them than they were scorned by the profane multitude, and their ministers were compelled to subscribe or be silent, and the poor people were persecuted ... they bore it all for several years in patience, until by the increase of their troubles they began to see further things by the light of the word of God. They realized not only that these base ceremonies were unlawful, but also that the tyrannous power of the prelates [Bishops] ought not to be submitted to, since it was contrary to the freedom of the gospel and would burden men's consciences and thus profane the worship of God ... Those reformers who saw the evil of these things, and whose hearts the Lord had touched with heavenly zeal for his truth, shook off this yoke of anti-Christian bondage, and as the Lord's free people joined themselves together by covenant as a church, in the fellowship of the gospel to walk in all his ways ... whatever it should cost them, the Lord assisting them. But after these things, they could not long continue in any peaceable condition, but were hunted and persecuted on every side, so as their former afflictions were but as flea-bitings in comparison of those which now came upon them. For some were taken and clapt up in prison; others had their houses beset and watched night and day, and hardly escaped their hands, and the most were fain to flee and leave their houses and habitations, and the means of their livelihoods.[1]

Fleeing from religious persecution in the Old World, they hoped to set up a godly nation in the New. Each town was built around the Congregational Church, and only church members could hold any civic position. Living a century after the arrival of these first settlers, Sarah and Jonathan Edwards were to be caught up in the tension caused as the growing population could not forever keep up this ideal of the Christian community.

By the 1700s, there were 13 small British colonies hugging the coast of the Atlantic. Jonathan and Sarah Edwards lived before Independence, and regarded themselves as British. The greater part of their life was spent in Northampton, a town of just over 1,000 inhabitants in the Connecticut River Valley. Its situation was pleasant: sheltered, with fertile land and beautiful scenery. It was also dangerous. Northampton was in a frontier area, continually vulnerable to attack, especially at times when England was at war with France: a conflict that spilled over from Europe to the colonies of both nations.

When Jonathan was born in 1703, the 'Sun King', Louis XIV of France, was still using military might to expand his territories. He was also brutally persecuting Protestants within his realm. In North America, the French encouraged Indians to attack English settlers. The year after Jonathan's birth, the infamous Deerfield massacre took place, just 50 miles north of where he was brought up in East Windsor. A joint French–Indian attack left 39 out of 300 inhabitants dead, and 112 taken prisoner. The victims included members of Jonathan's extended family: six-week-old Jerusha and six-year-old John died in the initial attack, their mother, Jonathan's relative, was killed when she could not keep up with the forced trek through deep snow to Canada, and their father and remaining siblings were kept captive in Canada.[2] Such memories were still fresh when Jonathan and Sarah started married life in Northampton 23 years later. Deerfield, the scene of that massacre, was just 16 miles away.

Nearly all the families worked the land. Men rose at dawn to work in the fields, or at the constant tasks of felling and cutting wood (for homes, furniture and fuel). Households were virtually self-sufficient. Many women wove cloth and made nearly all the goods needed by the family. There was only one general store for basic necessities. Occasional trips down to Boston or New York would be necessary for the purchase of other commodities. There was no mail service and no stagecoach. If you did have to travel, you travelled on horseback along the roughest of roads.

Life was hard, but sociable. The settlers chose to live close together, which ensured a tight-knit community life, with the church and school as the focal points. Nearly all the settlers would attend church. All men were expected to co-operate in the defence of the community. Each town was self-governing, a little democracy governed by the town hall meeting. The crime rate was virtually zero.

There was a marked gap between the wealthy and the poor. Church seating was determined by social status and society was strongly hierarchical. It was assumed that servants could be bought, sold and hired out to others.[3] A few (such as the Edwards' close friend Samuel Hopkins) viewed slavery as a horrible evil to be opposed. The majority, including Jonathan and Sarah, accepted it as part of the social structure of the day.[4] However, Jonathan was firmly convinced that:

In these two things, are contained the most forceable reasons against the master's abuse of his servant: That both have one Maker, and that their Maker made them alike with the same nature.[5]

Jonathan came to the point where he absolutely opposed the slave trade. He preached against any mistreatment of slaves. He regarded them as spiritually equal and was one of the first ministers to admit them to full church membership. His son, Jonathan Edwards Jr became a leading abolitionist, and used his father's writings to justify his stance. If Jonathan and Sarah had lived one generation later, they probably would have stood with their son on this issue.

Questions for reflection

1. During the seventeenth century, those who fled from England for conscientious reasons were determined 'to walk in all his [the Lord's] ways ... whatever it should cost them'. What motivates our decisions?

2. We shouldn't dismiss the legacy of people in the past when we disagree with some elements of their life. How can we cultivate gratitude for Christian leaders, while also being realistic about their limitations and failings?

2

Childhood: 'Joy unspeakable'

Sarah was born in 1710 in New Haven. Her father was a well-known minister, James Pierpont. Her mother, Mary (née Hooker), was the daughter and granddaughter of leading ministers. Sarah's family was one of the wealthiest and most respected in the colony. One of her great-grandfathers was Thomas Hooker, a founder of Connecticut, another was the first mayor of New York.

Sarah was four years old when her father died. Her mother stayed on in the church where he had ministered for the preceding 30 years. All descriptions of Sarah testify that she was beautiful, but more remarkable was her godliness, it is said that she 'exhibited the life and power of religion, and that in a remarkable manner, when only five years old'.[1]

She was only eight when Jonathan Edwards arrived in New Haven to study at the fledgling Yale College (of which her father had been one of the founders). Sarah's widowed mother had a prominent seat in the church, and it may have been in church that Jonathan first met this extraordinary child.

Five years later, in 1723, when Sarah was 13 and Jonathan 20, he penned the description of her that has passed into history. She delighted, he said, to walk alone in the country and think of God. She knew that this Creator God loved her personally and feared more than anything else to offend him. She loved to sing to God, and was often full of joy, sometimes unspeakable joy.

> *They say there is a young lady in New Haven who is loved by that Great Being, who made and rules the world, and that there are certain seasons in which this Great Being, in some way or other invisible, comes to her and fills her mind with exceeding sweet delight; and that she hardly cares for anything except to meditate on him ... She has a strange sweetness in her mind, and a singular purity in her affections, is most just and conscientious in her conduct, and you could not persuade her to do anything wrong or sinful if you would give her half the world, lest she should offend this Great Being. She is of a wonderful sweetness, calmness and universal benevolence of mind ... She will sometimes go about from place to place, singing sweetly, and seems always to be full of joy and pleasure and no one knows for what. She loves to be alone, walking in the fields and groves, and seems to have someone invisible always conversing with her.*[2]

Jonathan was enthralled, for he had discovered a kindred spirit. From an early age, he too had loved to wander alone in the woods and pray. He thought deeply about God, just as he thought deeply about everything. As a young tutor at Yale, he thought and wrote like a mature professor. No ordinary girl could have suited him, but Sarah was extraordinary. She was not disturbed by the profundity of his religious experience, for she shared it. She was not intimidated by his intellect – she too had received an excellent education. They were engaged when Sarah was just 15.[3] They shared a love of music and singing. They both admired the works of Isaac Watts (1674–1748), who had been revolutionising the enjoyment of public worship among the English dissenters, with his prolific compositions of hymns, and his renderings of Psalms (always viewed through the lens of the coming of Christ).[4]

A section from one of Sarah's diaries has been found, dated 22 October 1735. Written when she was 25 or so, she reflected on the way God had worked in her life when she was around 16:

> About nine years ago, I was led to see my danger of eternal destruction, but I had a resolution given me to seek for mercy … The words, 'Though he slay me, yet will I put my trust in him', often occurred to my mind. Not long after this, Isaiah 44:4–6 seemed to be God's call to me: 'This one will say, "I am the Lord's," another will call on the name of Jacob, and another will write on his hand, "The Lord's," and name himself by the name of Israel.'
>
> The next Sabbath I was led to prize nearness to Christ as the creature's greatest happiness. My soul thirsted for him, so that death seemed nothing to me, that I might be

with him; for he was altogether lovely. This frame of mind continued for some time.

The winter after, I had a greater sense of my own vileness than ever. I could truly say 'I abhorred myself and repented in dust and ashes.' It was not on account of the evil which sin would bring up on me, but because it dishonoured God. This view of sin had a great tendency to humble me, and to incline me to go to God for pardon. I had great confidence in my love to Christ, and was not afraid to appeal to him ... I loved Christ for what he was in himself; I loved him in all his offices; I saw my absolute need of him in all his offices,[5] and I thought I was as willing to be ruled by his laws as to be saved by his merits. I found a disposal to go to God as to a father. A soul-emptying and God-exalting way of being saved was what I greatly delighted in. The thoughts of my heart were, 'What have I that I have not received?' and 'Who hath made me to differ?' I felt a great love to the people of God, even if they were persons whom I had before disliked ... For half a year after I had very little fear of death ... It seemed almost impossible, that I should ever be in the least uneasy at anything I might meet with in the world; for all things were at the disposal of God.[6]

Sarah was already experiencing a deep desire that God should be glorified, and a profound sense of her need of Christ as her personal Saviour. She was convinced of the absolute sovereignty of God. In the light of that, she did not have to fear the future. At the age of 16, she was already convinced that 'nearness to Christ' is the greatest joy anyone can ever know. She knew that death, whenever it might come, would mean that she would finally be with Christ, the One who is 'altogether lovely'.

Questions for reflection:

1. 'I was led to prize nearness to Christ as the creature's greatest happiness.' Do you find joy in fellowship with the Triune God: Father, Son and Holy Spirit?

2. There are many examples in church history of children and teenagers demonstrating a profound knowledge of God. How do you think we might be in danger of underestimating the spiritual capacity of young people? Pray about how you could offer spiritual encouragement to the children and young people known to you.

3

Marriage: 'An uncommon union'

On 28 July 1727, 17-year-old Sarah married 25-year-old Jonathan. For the preceding five months, he had been co-pastor of the church at Northampton. The senior pastor, his grandfather Solomon Stoddard, had ministered there since 1669.

At 83, Stoddard was still a forceful preacher, and his church was one of the largest outside Boston. Stoddard's strength of character could lurch into dogmatism, a characteristic that rubbed off on his church members. There was a tendency to party division in Northampton. On one occasion, arguments in the church had even ended up with blows. Some years into his ministry, Jonathan reflected:

> It has been a very great wound to the church of
> Northampton, that there has been for forty or fifty years,

a sort of settled division of the people into two parties,
somewhat like the Court and Country party, in England
(if I may compare small things with great). There have been
some of the chief men in the town, of chief authority and
wealth, that have been great proprietors of their lands, who
have had one party with them. And the other party, which
has commonly been the greatest [in number], have been of
those, who have been jealous of them, apt to envy them,
and afraid of their having too much power and influence in
town and church.[1]

Despite this, all seemed reasonably peaceful when the young
Jonathan joined his grandfather. He does not seem to have
been intimidated by the large number of his own relatives in
the congregation. They in turn seem to have been impressed
with their new minister.

Sarah's entry into the church in Northampton in the
summer of 1727 was the focus of intense interest. She was
the first minister's wife to arrive there since the arrival of
Jonathan's grandmother in Northampton, in 1661. She was
expected to wear her wedding dress for her first Sunday
service. Custom dictated that she sit in a high seat in church
each Sunday, next to the pulpit and facing the congregation.
Self-control was called for, as any trace of boredom or tired-
ness would be obvious.

After a few months staying with Jonathan's grandparents,
the young couple moved into their own homestead, with 10
acres attached, and 40 acres of farmland further away. Parson-
ages at that time would have visitors constantly arriving and
expecting accommodation. Sarah created a warm, relaxed

and happy atmosphere in their home, which became prover-
bial for hospitality.

From the start of his ministry, Jonathan was unusual.
Other ministers were people-orientated; adept at relaxed conversation, seen regularly in the homes of their parishioners.
Many of them worked their own land. Jonathan Edwards was
one of the greatest intellects America has ever known, and
whatever else was going on around him he was focused on
thought, prayer, meditation and writing. He needed lengthy
periods of time to work through questions of theology and
philosophy. Parishioners with genuine problems knew they
could call on him, but he generally spent 13 or 14 hours each
day in his study. There was a sense of destiny about this. God
had gifted him with a capacity to push forward the frontiers
of thought. He had a solemn obligation to use the talent he
had been given.

Time spent in his study was not spent in merely academic
studies. For Jonathan Edwards, the essential and central business of life is to know God, to seek God's face and to enjoy
fellowship with him:

> *The enjoyment of God is the only true happiness with*
> *which our souls can be satisfied. To go to heaven, fully*
> *to enjoy God, is infinitely better than the most pleasant*
> *accommodations here. Fathers and mothers, husbands,*
> *wives or children, or the company of earthly friends, are but*
> *shadows; but God is the substance. These are but scattered*
> *beams, but God is the sun. These are but streams, but God is*
> *the ocean.*[2]

As a young man, he wrote:

> *I felt a burning desire to be ... conformed to the blessed image of Christ ... . It was my continual strife, day and night, and constant daily enquiry, how I should be more holy, and live more holily, and more becoming a child of God, and a disciple of Christ.*[3]

Jonathan devised a series of resolutions, which expressed his desire for deeper godliness. Among them:

> *Resolved, never to do any manner of thing, whether in soul or body, less or more, but what tends to the glory of God ...*
>
> *Resolved, to live with all my might, while I do live.*
>
> *Resolved, never to lose one moment of time; but improve it the most profitable way I possibly can.*
>
> *Resolved, never to do anything, which I should be afraid to do, if it were the last hour of my life.*
>
> *Resolved, in narrations never to speak anything but the pure and simple verity.*
>
> *Resolved, never to speak evil of any, except I have some particular good call for it.*[4]

As a youngster, Jonathan had for a while resisted (even hated) the biblical teaching of God's sovereignty. But he came to rejoice in it:

I had a very affecting sense, how meet and suitable it was that God should govern the world, and order all things according to his own pleasure, and I rejoiced in it, that God reigned, and that his will was done.[5]

After he took up ministry at Northampton he wrote:

I have often had sweet complacency in God, in views of his glorious perfections and the excellency of Jesus Christ. God has appeared to me a glorious and lovely Being, chiefly on account of his holiness. The holiness of God has always appeared to me as the most lovely of all his attributes ... The gospel has seemed to me the richest treasure; the treasure that I have most desired, and longed that it may dwell richly in me ... And God has appeared glorious to me on account of the Trinity ... Once, as I rode out into the woods for my health ... I had a view that for me was extraordinary, of the glory of the Son of God, as Mediator between God and man, and his wonderful, great, full, pure, and sweet grace and love, and meek and gentle condescension ... The person of Christ appeared ineffably excellent with an excellency great enough to swallow up all thought and conception – which continued about an hour; which kept me the greater part of that time in a flood of tears and weeping aloud. I felt an ardency of soul to be ... emptied and annihilated; to lie in the dust and be full of Christ alone; to love Him with a holy and pure love; to trust in Him; to live upon Him; to serve and follow Him; and to be perfectly sanctified and made pure, with a divine and heavenly purity.[6]

As a young man, Jonathan worked out a regime of diet, exercise and sleep by which he could achieve maximum mental efficiency. He followed this for the rest of his life. It required self-discipline, as he was often ill. He got up each day at about 5 am. Sarah fitted in with his hours, cared for the visitors and organised domestic arrangements. She managed the home and farm. By taking charge of practical things, she freed Jonathan for his calling.

Jonathan spent long hours in the study, but he would take a break during the afternoon, sometimes riding out into the country with Sarah. An hour each evening was spent with the family.

Sarah shared her husband's eternal perspective and sense of destiny. Jonathan was not studying for the sake of it. He was convinced that this world is created for a purpose: God's own glory. The establishment of the kingdom of Christ on earth is the means by which this is achieved. While still 19 years old, he had written:

> *I had great longings for the advancement of Christ's kingdom in the world; and my secret prayers used to be, in great part, taken up in praying for it. If I heard the least hint of anything that happened in any part of the world, that appeared in some respect or other, to have a favourable aspect on the interests of Christ's kingdom, my soul eagerly catched at it, and it would much animate and refresh me. I used to be eager to read public news-letters, mainly for that end: to see if I could not see some news favourable to the interest of religion in the world.*[7]

His endeavours in writing and preaching were one little part of the establishment of Christ's kingdom. Sarah's support of his ministry was not only a sign of her love for her husband, she regarded it as service to her God.

This service had nothing gloomy or threatening about it. The heart of their religion was love. Heaven, wrote Jonathan, is a 'world of love', and Christians are to begin to live a life of love here too. Christianity is only genuine if there is affection, patience and generosity towards others. Jonathan was a loving husband; Sarah was a loving wife. The great love of God towards them, they believed, demanded no less.

On his deathbed, Jonathan sent word to Sarah that the 'uncommon union' they had enjoyed could not be broken by death. They would love each other through all eternity. Theirs was indeed an 'uncommon union'. Two extraordinary people, devoted to God and to each other.

Questions for reflection

1. Consider the resolutions Jonathan Edwards framed, and also the deep joy in God that he experienced. What was the connection?

2. How did Sarah and Jonathan complement each other?

3. What was the priority in their marriage?

4

Motherhood:
A role of eternal significance

Sarah married at 17, had her first baby the next year, and had ten more children at approximately two-year intervals until she was 40. The last was born in 1750. Eight were daughters, the first one named Sarah. Just before their second daughter was born, in 1729, Jonathan had visited his parental home in East Windsor. It was the last time he would ever see his 19-year-old sister, Jerusha. She had shown profound godliness from a young age, and died testifying to God's grace:

> ... to her, no society was so delightful as solitude with God. She read theology with deepest interest ... There were occasions in her Christian life when her experience could be best described in a line from Isaac Watts: 'And sudden from

*the cleaving skies, a gleam of glory broke.' And so it was
to be at the end. A day or two before her death in December
1729, as she contemplated God's grace in Christ, she
exclaimed to herself, 'It is wonderful, it surprises me.'*[1]

Unsurprising, then, that when a second child was born to
Jonathan and Sarah in the following April, they named her
Jerusha. Their fifth daughter, born in August 1736 was named
Lucy, in honour of another of Jonathan's sisters, who died
earlier that month aged 21.

Sarah, Jerusha, Esther, Mary, Lucy, Timothy, Susannah,
Eunice, Jonathan, Elizabeth and Pierpont all survived infancy,
which was unusual in an age of high infant mortality. At this
time, there were also high rates of maternal death. Sarah
nearly lost her life during at least one confinement.

Jonathan and Sarah's great-grandson, Sereno Edwards
Dwight, included this glowing tribute to Sarah in his *Memoir*
written in 1830:

*No person of discernment could be conversant in the family,
without observing and admiring the perfect harmony and
mutual love and esteem that existed between them [Sarah
and Jonathan] ... when she herself laboured under bodily
disorders and pains, which was not infrequently the case,
instead of troubling those around her with her complaints,
and wearing a sour and dejected countenance, as if out of
humour with every body, and every thing around her ...
she was accustomed to bear up under them, not only with
patience but with cheerfulness and good humour ... She had
an excellent way of governing her children: she knew how*

*to make them regard and obey her cheerfully, without loud
angry words, much less, heavy blows. She seldom punished
them, and in speaking to them used gentle and pleasant
words. If any correction was needed, she did not administer
it in a passion; and when she had occasion to reprove and
rebuke, she would do it in few words, without warmth and
noise, and with all calmness and gentleness of mind. In
her directions and reproofs in matters of importance she
would address herself to the reason of her children, that
they might not only know her inclination and will, but
at the same time be convinced of the reasonableness of it.
She had need to speak but once; she was cheerfully obeyed;
murmuring and answering again were not know among
them. They were uncommonly respectful to their parents.[2]*

Sarah's domestic responsibilities were unremitting. She had
help in the house, but that was a necessity when everything
had to be done at home – making butter and cheese, spin-
ning, even making up bedsteads each year, taking the frames
apart and filling them with fresh straw. Sarah, like any other
woman, found her physical energy depleted with frequent
pregnancy and nursing. In the winter of 1740 when she was
30, she and all the children (then aged 12, 10, 8, 6, 4, 2 and six
months) had measles. In the summer of 1750, she succumbed
to rheumatic fever.

Jonathan believed that girls as well as boys should receive a
thorough education. He had grown up alongside ten sisters,
who had all been taught Latin and other subjects.[3] The Edwards
daughters were educated at home, the sons attended school.
Daily family worship, along with visitors and those working

in the home, took place morning and evening. Psalms and the 'new' hymns being written by English hymn-writer Isaac Watts were sung. Jonathan believed that teaching children to sing, and equipping them to sing in parts in congregational worship, was an essential part of their education.[4]

We catch a glimpse of Sarah in the everyday routine of motherhood from the first-hand accounts written by some of the Edwards' guests. One mid-winter's day in 1741, when Jonathan was away, a stranger arrived on the doorstep. Young Samuel Hopkins was going through a spiritual crisis and wanted advice from Jonathan. Sarah was then 31, and the seven children ranged from 13 down to 18 months. She welcomed Samuel in. He ended up staying for the whole winter and would become a regular visitor and a firm family friend. He testified to Sarah's love for her family, and her excellent management of the home. She was in absolute control of her children – the norm of the time was implicit obedience – but there was also affection and fun. Day-to-day life was pleasant in their home. Amid the business of looking after the children, she took time to speak to Samuel about his spiritual anxieties. When Jonathan arrived home, Samuel noted the deep love between husband and wife.

Other guests supported this testimony. The famous English preacher George Whitefield stayed with them in 1740, the year before Samuel Hopkins' arrival. He too was impressed with the harmonious atmosphere in their home. He too was especially taken with Sarah, noting in his journal his prayer that God would provide him a partner just like her.

Motherhood was, however, physically and emotionally draining. Jonathan wrote that in the early years of motherhood, Sarah was often tense, tired and fearful: 'subject to unsteadiness, and many ups and downs, in the frame of mind, being under great disadvantages, through a vaporous habit of body, and often subject to melancholy, and at times almost over-borne with it, having been so even from early youth'.[5] When she was physically weak, she was more prone to anxiety. Childbirth was not only painful, but dangerous. Then there were the physical demands of nursing, broken sleep, caring for little ones through illness, and the daily work of teaching and training them.

Sarah drew strength from spiritual resources. She knew that each of her children had an eternal soul and she longed, by God's grace, that each would serve him for ever. When her daughter Esther was pregnant with her first child, Sarah reminded her of the 'sacred privilege' of motherhood. Even if a child were to die in infancy, it was worthwhile going through pregnancy and labour. The infant would have an exalted eternal destiny. Esther remembered that her mother viewed each pregnancy as a gift from God. Sarah had prayed for, and with, each of her children.

Amidst all the demands of motherhood, Sarah drew strength from her certain assurance of the love and care of God. She came to the point where she handed everything over to God – life or death, health or sickness, wealth or poverty, popularity or rejection. In around 1735, aged 25, Sarah was evidently enabled to resign all to God and trust in his sovereign goodness. After that time, Jonathan wrote, this 'resignation of all ... wholly conquered these disadvan-tages [the weakness and depression], and carried the mind in a constant manner, quite above all such effects'.[6] Sarah had 'remained in a constant uninterrupted rest' since then, but she was given an even deeper assurance in early 1742 (when she was 32). This would be tested by a series of tragedies. Sarah continued to trust God's sovereignty and love through them all.

Of Jonathan and Sarah's children, all except Jerusha (who died aged 17) and Elizabeth (who died aged 14) survived to adulthood. In 1900, a survey was made of the Edwards' descendants. From their marriage had come a large number of people who had made a variety of contributions to society: clergymen, lawyers, professors, politicians, businessmen, doctors and 100 missionaries. The most high-profile was Aaron Burr, who became vice president of the United States.[7] The author of the survey concluded: 'much of the capacity and talent, intensity and character of the more than 1,400 of the Edwards family is due to Mrs Edwards'.[8]

Questions for reflection

1. Motherhood presented many challenges for Sarah Edwards. How did she respond to them?

2. What does this teach us today?

PART 2

Delighting in God

So I have looked upon you in the sanctuary,
beholding your power and glory.
Because your steadfast love is better than life,
my lips will praise you.

So I will bless you as long as I live;
in your name I will lift up my hands.

My soul will be satisfied as with fat and rich food,
and my mouth will praise you with joyful lips.

Psalm 63:2–5

5

Revival (1734-42): 'Uninterrupted cheerfulness, peace and joy'

Jonathan Edwards took over as the senior minister at Northampton in 1729 when his grandfather, Solomon Stoddard died. Sarah was an enthusiastic participant in women's prayer meetings, and visited the poor, the sick and the bereaved.[1] We know that Jonathan Edwards believed in the duty of giving generously to the poor.[2] Sarah was given ample scope to minister to the needy of the parish. Her third daughter Esther kept a diary indicating that, after the birth of her own children, she also was active in such visiting. We can be sure that she was following the example her mother had set.

An unhelpful result of equating church and community was that the minister and his wife were put up on a pedestal. They were accorded a high social status within the town, which meant that Sarah was the object of general scrutiny. This must have been difficult when she was suffering from nervous and physical exhaustion. Sunday after Sunday she had to put on a brave face and sit in full view of the congregation.[3] But the Edwards were caught up in a social structure that they were powerless to change. Some of this is reflected in the way that Sarah was sensitive to how people in the community judged her. A fresh experience of God's love for her would, in time, liberate her from this pressure.

During the first six years in Northampton Sarah settled into the community. As she made acquaintance with her husband's numerous relations, she discovered that relationships in the large extended family were not always harmonious. In 1734, Jonathan found himself taking the opposite side in a theological conflict to one of his numerous cousins. Israel Williams, then aged just 25, never forgave Jonathan. His hostility would trouble Jonathan for the rest of his life.

When Jonathan had arrived in Northampton, most of the inhabitants attended church, but many were far from born again. The majority of young people were worldly, with low moral standards. Seven years after his arrival, in 1734, one young man died just two days after contracting a violent illness. This shocked the small community.[4] Jonathan seized the opportunity. At the funeral, he preached on Psalm 90:5–6: 'In the morning they are like grass which groweth up … In the evening it is cut down and withereth.' All the young people of the town were at the funeral and he challenged them directly:

> *... how unreasonable it is for one who is so much like the grass and flowers of the field ... to spend away the prime of his opportunity in levity and vain mirth ... Consider: if you should die in youth how shocking would the thought of your having spent your youth in such a manner ... When others stand by your bedside and see you gasping and breathing your last ... how shocking it will be to them to think this is the person that used to be so vain and frothy in conversation* [5]

Later, in a meeting for the young people, Jonathan continued to urge them to think of eternity. Soon, instead of the socialising that had been taking place after public worship, groups of youngsters were meeting for earnest prayer. During the spring of 1735, many came under intense conviction of sin, and then to a personal knowledge of forgiveness.

It was not just young people. Jonathan Edwards reported that he was seeing 30 conversions a week. Three hundred people were converted in a six-month period – the first revival of his ministry.

Excitement in the town was intense. Jonathan and Sarah found their home crowded with people wanting spiritual advice. Many who had been nominal Christians were now personally convinced of spiritual realities. Those who were already genuine believers enjoyed a fresh sense of the presence of God. Jonathan Edwards wrote that during 1735:

> *Our public assemblies were then beautiful; the congregation was alive in God's service, everyone was earnestly intent on the public worship, every hearer eager to drink in the words*

of the minister as they came from his mouth; the assembly
in general were, from time to time in tears while the Word
was preached; some weeping with sorrow and distress,
others with joy and love, others with pity and concern for
the souls of their neighbours. Our public praises were then
greatly enlivened; God was then served in our psalmody,
in some measure in the beauty of holiness ... there has
been scarce any part of divine worship, wherein good men
amongst us have had grace so drawn forth, and their hearts
so lifted up, as in singing his praises.[6]

Northampton was not the only town affected. Similar scenes took place throughout Connecticut, and further afield. A series of conversions was reported in Dutch Reformed churches in New Jersey in 1726. Many Presbyterian and Congregationalist churches also saw dramatic increases in membership. Those who had been nominal church attenders found themselves gripped by conviction of sin, and then wonderfully assured of their personal salvation.

Jonathan was overjoyed, but he soon had to cope with the downside of revival. The mood of Northampton darkened with an appalling suicide: that of Jonathan's uncle, Joseph Hawley, one of the most prominent citizens of Northampton. Jonathan tried to comfort his bereaved aunt, and to provide help to his two fatherless cousins. It would be one of these young men (Joseph Hawley Jr) who would eventually take the leading role in opposition to Jonathan.

The immediate result of the revival was an increased congregation. Work began on a new meeting house, next to the old one, in the summer of 1736. The spring thaw in March

1737 weakened the old structure. One Sunday morning, while Jonathan was preaching, the entire gallery collapsed while full of people. Miraculously there were no fatalities.

The new meeting house, with seating for 800, was used for the first time on 25 December 1737 (Edwards along with many Puritans did not celebrate Christmas Day). Much debate took place over the seating plan, which was arranged according to social standing. For a town that had experienced the grace of God in revival to argue over this issue seemed incongruous. Jonathan Edwards told them so in no uncertain terms in the opening sermon.

Although the rate of conversions slowed down, the mood of the town continued to be 'serious' and a good number of people met for prayer. The young people were more religiously minded than they had been for decades. The year 1740 marked the height of the revival movement throughout New England. Congregations began to experience outward excitement. A sense of the presence of the holy God caused many to cry out aloud due to conviction of sin and fear of judgement. Some fainted; many wept.

In the autumn of 1740, the English evangelist George Whitefield visited New England. Huge crowds gathered to hear him preach. In Boston, he preached outdoors to a crowd of 20,000 – the largest audience ever gathered at that time in the colonies.[7]

Nathan Cole, a New England farmer, described what happened one morning, when he got word that George Whitefield was due to preach at 10 am, 12 miles from where he lived:

I was in my field, at work, I dropped my tool that was in my hand and ran home and ran through the house and bid my wife to get ready quick to go and hear Mr Whitefield preach at Middletown and ran to my pasture for my horse with all my might, fearing I should be too late to hear him. I brought my horse home and soon mounted and took my wife up and went forward as fast as I thought the horse could bear, and when my horse began to be out of breath I would get down and put my wife in the saddle and bid her ride as fast as she could and not stop or slack for me except I bade her, and so I would run until I was almost out of breath and then mount my horse again, and so I did several times to favour my horse ... for we had 12 miles to ride double in little more than an hour. On high ground I saw before me a cloud or fog rising, I first thought off from a great river but as I came nearer the road I heard a noise something like a low rumbling of horses feet coming down the road and this cloud was a cloud of dust made by the running of horses' feet. It arose some rods in the air, over the tops of hills and trees, and when I came within about twenty rods of the road I could see men and horses slipping along in the cloud like shadows and when I came nearer it was like a steady stream of horses and their riders, scarcely a horse more than his length behind another, all of a lather and some with sweat.

We went down with the stream, I heard no man speak a word all the way, three miles, but everyone pressing forward with great haste, and when we got down to the old meeting house there was a great multitude – it was said to be 3

> *or 4,000 people assembled together. We got off from our*
> *horses and shook off the dust, and the ministers were then*
> *coming to the meetinghouse. I turned and looked towards*
> *the great river and saw ferry boats running swift, forward*
> *and backward, bringing over loads of people, the oars*
> *rowed nimble and quick. Everything, men, horses and boats*
> *all seemed to be struggling for life, the land and the banks*
> *over the river looked all black with people and horses. All*
> *along the 12 miles I saw no man at work in his field, but all*
> *seemed to be gone.*[8]

Jonathan Edwards invited Whitefield to visit Northampton. As well as preaching in the church, Whitefield spoke in the Edwards' home to their older children, then aged 12, 10, 8, 6 and 4.[9] The following spring, Jonathan wrote: 'this winter has been a time of the most remarkable and visible blessing of heaven upon my family that ever there was'. He believed that 'my four eldest children have been savingly wrought upon'.[10]

During 1741, one of the significant results of revival in Northampton was the conversion of many of the children and young people in the town. By this time, Jonathan was receiving many invitations from outside his own church. In July 1741, he preached a sermon in nearby Enfield: 'Sinners in the Hands of an Angry God'. He had preached this sermon already in Northampton, but on this occasion it had an extraordinarily powerful impact. Many in Enfield were deeply convicted of sin, crying out loud in fear of judgement, or weeping repentant tears.

In January 1742, a young visiting preacher by the name of Samuel Buell came to supply the pulpit in Northampton when Jonathan was away preaching. Buell's preaching led to many people in Northampton (including Sarah) experiencing powerful spiritual impressions. This was the last year they were to experience revival.

The revival had caused bitter division among the ministers of New England. Around a third of them dismissed it as merely human emotion and mass hysteria. Jonathan Edwards was realistic enough to understand this reaction. He agreed that a dramatic 'conversion experience' was meaningless unless it resulted in a life of obedience. Indeed, it could be worse than useless, because the excitement of the 'experience' led some individuals to believe that they were infallible. 'Revival' could overflow into fanaticism. Heightened excitement could lead people into actions that were misguided, while they claimed to be under the guidance of the Holy Spirit. Some were thrilled by the notion that God would speak directly to them but made ridiculous claims. Others condemned mature leaders as lacking the Spirit. When Jonathan reflected on those months in 1735 when so many were professing faith in Northampton, he accepted that only time could determine how many of those professions were genuine.

Yet the presence of the false did not negate the presence of the true. The revival contained good and bad. He set out to analyse the unusual scenes that had resulted from this phenomenon called 'revival'. And he had a case study in his own home. Sarah, too, had had an extraordinary experience. When he returned from a preaching engagement early in 1742, the whole town was wondering whether she would even survive until his return. She had been prostrated physically with religious ecstasy, and for days and nights at a time had been overwhelmed with a powerful sense of the love of God.

Jonathan wanted to evaluate what had happened. He asked Sarah to sit down and describe every detail. She gave him a precise account of her spiritual experience that had lasted from 19 January to 11 February 1742.

When Jonathan came to record this description, he put it in context. During the preceding years, Sarah had been desiring God and seeking holiness. She had submitted to God in times of pain, she had battled temptation, she had used the means of grace (prayer, listening to preaching, reading the Word, spiritual conversation, and engaging in works of mercy and service). Her experience of 1742 was the answer to many years of prayer that she would know God's smile. As Jonathan wrote:

> *Mrs Edwards had been long, in an uncommon manner,*
> *growing in grace and rising by very sensible degrees to*
> *higher love to God, weanedness from the world, and*
> *mastery over sin and temptation, through great trials*
> *and conflicts, and long-continued struggling and fighting*
> *with sin, and earnest and constant prayer and labour in*
> *religion, and engagedness of mind in the use of all means,*
> *attended with a great exactness of life; and this growth had*
> *been attended not only with a great increase of religious*
> *affections, but with a most visible alteration of outward*
> *behaviour; particularly in living above the world, and a*
> *greater degree of steadfastness and strength in the way of*
> *duty and self-denial: maintaining the Christian conflict*
> *against temptations, and conquering from time to time*
> *under great trials; persisting in an unmoved, untouched*

calm and rest, under the changes and accidents of time,
such as seasons of extreme pain and apparent hazard of
immediate death.

These transports did not arise from bodily weakness,
but were greatest in the best state of health. They were
accompanied with a lively sense of the greatness of God,
and her own littleness and vileness, and had abiding effects
in the increase of the sweetness, rest and humility which
they left upon the soul, and in a new engagedness of heart,
to live to the honour of God, and to watch and fight against
sin. They were attended with no enthusiastical disposition
to follow impulses or supposed revelations, nor with any
appearance of spiritual pride; but on the contrary, with
a very great increase of meekness and humility, and a
disposition in honour to prefer others, as well as with a
great aversion to judging others, and a strong sense of the
importance of moral, social duties.[11]

It is a mark of revivals through history that at such times
Christians become powerfully aware that what may seem to
be 'small' sins are infinitely offensive to the holy God. Sarah
became convinced that her desire for her husband and herself
to be well thought of by others, and her dependence on
Jonathan's good opinion, were profoundly sinful. She became
more intensely aware that God's verdict alone really matters.
The things she had previously feared most: the ill will of the
town, or the disapproval of her husband, would now mean
nothing to her. She became aware of an entire resignation
to God's will: willing to die any death, and, even more of a

test, willing to live for him. She imagined her 'worst-case' scenarios, and felt that she would, through them all, be able to assent with 'Yes, Lord Jesus, Amen, Lord Jesus', and she was filled with intense love for others.

Jonathan concluded that Sarah's experience had been the most intense, pure, unmixed and well-regulated of any he had seen during the revival. He saw that the effect in her life was remarkable. Throughout all the trials that confronted them during the coming months and years, he could bear witness to her continued peace, cheerfulness and joy.

Questions for reflection

1. What did Sarah Edwards seek through years of prayer?

2. Reflect on Sarah's conviction that what may seem to be 'small' sins are infinitely offensive to our holy God (Psalms 19:12–13; 139:23–24).

6

Testimony: 'My God, my all'

For just over three weeks, from 19 January to 11 February 1742, Sarah, aged 32, had a deeper experience of the presence of God than anything she had known previously. Much of that time Jonathan had been away on a preaching trip. Many other parishioners were also finding their spiritual lives revived under the ministry of Samuel Buell, a young visiting preacher. During those weeks the Edwards' home was often filled with people meeting for spiritual conversation, Bible readings and prayer.

Jonathan wrote down her account of what had happened, and included it his book, *Some Thoughts Concerning the Present Revival of Religion in New England, and the Way in Which it Ought to Be Acknowledged and Promoted*.[1] But he concealed his wife's identity, saying only that a 'person of discretion' had shared their experience with him. The testimony was not published under Sarah's name until after her death.

Thoughts Concerning the Present Revival was written in order to help people distinguish between the true and the false in the 'present revival'. Many had denounced revival as fanaticism, on the basis of individual examples of hysteria or excess. Jonathan argued rather that 'the extraordinary work which has of late been going on in this land is a *glorious work of God*'. He entitled the fifth section 'The nature of the work in a particular instance', and here provided Sarah's account as the most pure and genuine instance he had witnessed of extraordinary enjoyment of God.[2]

The account is long, and there is some repetition. But as you read it I would encourage you to look for and highlight the following recurring themes:

1. Desire for greater holiness

2. Submission of all to God

3. Desire for God's glory

4. Joyful assurance of God's love and forgiveness: an anticipation of heaven

5. Intense love for others: unwillingness to have any judgemental thoughts

Testimony of Sarah Edwards, 19 January – 11 February 1742[3]

Tuesday night January 19, 1742. *I felt very uneasy and unhappy, at my being so low in grace. I thought I very much needed help from God, and found a spirit of*

*earnestness to seek help of him that I might have more
holiness. When I had for a time been earnestly wrestling
with God for it, I felt within myself great quietness of spirit,
unusual submission to God, and willingness to wait upon
him, with respect to the time and manner in which he
should help me, and wished that he should take his own
time and his own way, to do it.*

*The next morning (**Wednesday January 20, 1742**) I
found a great uneasiness in my mind, at Mr Edwards's
suggesting, that he thought I had failed in some measure
of prudence, in some conversation I had had with Mr
Williams, of Hadley, the day before. I found that it seemed
to bereave me of the quietness and calm of my mind, in
any respect not to have the good opinion of my husband.
This I much disliked in myself, as arguing a want of
sufficient rest in God, and felt a disposition to fight against
it, and look to God for his help, that I might have a more
full and entire rest in him, independent of all other things.
I continued in this frame, from early in the morning until
about 10 o'clock, at which time the Rev. Mr Reynolds went
to prayer in the family.*

*I had, before this, so entirely given myself up to God, and
resigned up everything into his hands, that I had, for a long
time, felt myself quite alone in this world; so that the peace
and calm of my mind, and my rest in God as my only and
all sufficient happiness, seemed sensibly above the reach of
any disturbance, from anything but these two:*

1st, my own name and fair reputation among men, and especially the esteem and just treatment of the people of this town.

2nd, and more particularly the esteem, and love, and kind treatment of my husband.

At times, indeed, I had seemed to be considerably elevated above the influence of even these things; yet I had not found my calm, and peace, and rest in God so sensibly, fully and constantly, above the reach of disturbance from them, until now.

While Mr Reynolds was at prayer in the family this morning, I felt an earnest desire that, in calling on God, he should say, 'Father', or that he should address the Almighty under that appellation: on which the thought turneth in my mind – 'Why can I say, Father? – Can I now, at this time, with the confidence of a child, and without the least misgiving of heart, call God my Father?' This brought to mind two lines of Mr Erskine's sonnet:

*'I see him lay his vengeance by,
And smile in Jesus' face'*[4]

I was thus deeply sensible, that my sins did loudly call for vengeance, but I then by faith saw God 'lay his vengeance by, and smile in Jesus' face'. It appeared to me real and certain that he did so. I had not the least doubt, that he then sweetly smiled upon me, with the look of forgiveness

*and love, having laid aside all his displeasure towards
me, for Jesus' sake; which made me feel very weak and
somewhat faint.*

*In consequence of this, I felt a strong desire to be alone
with God, to go to him, without having anyone to interrupt
the silent and soft communion, which I earnestly desired
between God and my own soul; and accordingly withdrew
to my chamber.*

*It should have been mentioned that, before I retired, while
Mr Reynolds was praying, these words in Romans 8:34
came into my mind, 'Who is he that condemneth, it is
Christ that died, yea rather that is risen again, who is even
at the right hand of God, who also maketh intercession
for us' as well as the following words 'Who shall separate
us from the love of Christ?' &c, which occasioned great
sweetness and delight in my soul.*

*But when I was alone, the words came to my mind with far
greater power and sweetness; upon which I took the Bible
and read the words to the end of the chapter, when they
were impressed on my heart with vastly greater power
and sweetness still. They appeared to me with undoubted
certainty as the words of God, and as words which God did
pronounce concerning me. I had no more doubt of it than I
had of my being.*

*I seemed to hear the great God proclaiming thus to the
world concerning me; 'Who shall lay anything to thy*

charge' &c. and had it strongly impressed on me, how impossible it was for anything in heaven or on earth, in this world or the future, ever to separate me from the love of God which was in Christ Jesus.

I cannot find language to express, how certain this appeared – the everlasting mountains and hills were but shadows to it. My safety, and happiness, and eternal enjoyment of God's immutable love, seemed as durable and unchangeable as God himself. Melted and overcome by the sweetness of this assurance, I fell into a great flow of tears, and could not forbear weeping aloud. It appeared certain to me that God was my Father, and Christ my Lord and Saviour, that he was mine, and I his.

Under a delightful sense of the immediate presence and love of God, these words seemed to come over and over again in my mind, 'My God, my all; my God, my all.'

The presence of God was so near and so real, that I seemed scarcely conscious of anything else. God the Father, and the Lord Jesus, seemed as distinct persons, both manifesting their inconceivable loveliness and mildness and gentleness, and their great and immutable love to me. I seemed to be taken under the care and charge of my God and Saviour in an inexpressibly endearing manner; and Christ appeared to me as a mighty Saviour, under the character of the Lion of the tribe of Judah, taking my heart, with all its corruptions, under his care, and putting it at his feet.

Testimony: 'My God, my all'

In all things which concerned me, I felt myself safe, under the protection of the Father and Saviour; who appeared with supreme kindness to keep a record of everything I did, and of everything that was done to me, purely for my good.

The peace and happiness which I hereupon felt, was altogether inexpressible. It seemed to be that which came from heaven; to be eternal and unchangeable. I seemed to be lifted above earth and hell, out of the reach of everything here below, so that I could look upon all the rage and enmity of men or devils, with a kind of holy indifference, and an undisturbed tranquillity.

At the same time, I felt compassion and love for all mankind, and a deep abasement of soul, under a sense of my own unworthiness. I thought of the ministers who were in the house, and felt willing to undergo any labour and self-denial, if they would but come to the help of the Lord.

I also felt myself more perfectly weaned from all things here below, than ever before. The whole world, with all its enjoyments and all its troubles, seemed to be nothing. My God was my all, my only portion. No possible suffering seemed worth regarding: all persecutions and torments were a mere nothing. I seemed to dwell on high, and the place of defence to be the munition[5] of rocks.

After some time, the two evils mentioned above, as those which I should have been least able to bear, came to my mind – the ill treatment of the town, and the ill will of my husband; but now I was carried exceedingly above even such things as these, and I could feel that if I were exposed to them both, they would seem competitively nothing.

There was then a deep snow on the ground, and I could think of being driven away from my home into the cold and snow, of being chased from the town with the utmost contempt and malice, and of being left to perish with the cold, as cast out by all the world, with perfect calmness and serenity. It appeared to me, that it would not move me, or in the least disturb the inexpressible happiness and peace of my soul. My mind seemed as much above all things, as the sun is above the earth.

I continued in a very sweet and lively sense of divine things, day and night, waking and sleeping, until **Saturday, January 23, 1742.** *On Saturday morning, I had a most solemn and deep impression on my mind of the eye of God as fixed upon me, to observe what improvement I made of those spiritual communications I received from him; as well as the respect shown Mr Edwards, who had then been sent for to preach at Leicester. I was sensible that I was sinful enough to bestow it on my pride, or on my sloth, which seemed exceedingly dreadful to me.*

At night my soul seemed to be filled with an inexpressibly sweet and pure love to God, and to the children of God, with a refreshing consolation and solace of soul, which made me willing to lie on the earth, at the feet of the servants of God,

to declare his gracious dealings with me, and breathe forth
before them my love, and gratitude and praise.

Sabbath January 24, 1742. I enjoyed a sweet, and lively,
and assured sense of God's infinite grace and favour, and
love to me, in taking me out of the depths of hell, and
exalting me to the heavenly glory, and the dignity of a royal
priesthood.

Monday night January 25, 1742. Mr Edwards, being
gone that day to Leicester, I heard that Mr Buell was
coming to the town, and from what I had heard of him and
of his success, I had strong hopes that there would be great
effects from his labours here.

At the same time, I had a deep and affecting impression,
that the eye of God was ever on my heart, and that it
greatly concerned me to watch my heart, and see to it
that I was perfectly resigned to God, with respect to the
instruments he should make use of to revive religion in
this town, and be entirely willing, if it was God's good
pleasure, that he should make use of Mr Buell; and
also that other Christians should appear to excel me in
Christian experience, and in the benefit they should derive
from ministers.

I was conscious, that it would be exceedingly provoking
to God if I should not be thus resigned, and earnestly
endeavoured to watch my heart, that no feelings of a
contrary nature might arise; and was enabled, as I thought,

to exercise full resignation, and acquiescence in God's pleasure, as to these things.

I was sensible what great cause I had to bless God for the use he had made of Mr Edwards hitherto; but thought if he never blessed his labours any more, and should greatly bless the labours of other ministers, I could completely acquiesce in his will.

It appeared to me meet and proper, that God should employ babes and sucklings to advance his kingdom. When I thought of these things it was my instinctive feeling to say 'Amen, Lord Jesus! Amen, Lord Jesus!' This seemed to be the sweet and instinctive language of my soul.

*On **Tuesday (January 26, 1742)** I remained in a sweet and lively exercise of this resignation, and love to and rest in God, seeming to be in my heart day by day, far above the reach of anything here below. On Tuesday night, especially the latter part of it, I felt a great earnestness of soul and engagedness in seeking God for the town, that religion might now revive, and that God would bless Mr Buell to that end. God seemed to be very near to me while I was thus striving with him for these things, and I had a strong hope that what I sought of him would be granted. There seemed naturally and unavoidably to arise in my mind an assurance that God would now do great things for Northampton.*

*On **Wednesday morning (January 27, 1742)** I heard that Mr Buell arrived the night before at Mr Phelps's, and that* *there seemed to be great tokens and effects of the presence of God there which greatly encouraged and rejoiced me. About an hour and a half after, Mr Buell came to our house; I sat still in entire resignedness to God, and willingness that God should bless his labours here as much as he pleased; though it be for the enlivening of every saint, and to the conversion of every sinner, in the town.*

These feelings continued afterwards, when I saw his great success; as I never felt the least rising of heart to the contrary, but my submission was even and uniform, without any interruption or disturbance. I rejoiced when I saw the honour which God placed upon him, and the respect paid him by the people, and the greater success following his preaching than had followed the preaching of Mr Edwards immediately before he went to Leicester. I found rest and rejoicing in it, and the sweet language of my soul continually was 'Amen, Lord Jesus! Amen, Lord Jesus!'

At 3 o'clock in the afternoon, a lecture was preached by Mr Buell. In the latter part of the sermon, one or two appeared much moved, and after the blessing, when the people were going out, several others. To my mind, there was the clearest evidence that God was present in the congregation, on the work of redeeming love; and in a clear view of this, I was all at once filled with such intense admiration of the wonderful condescension and grace of God, in returning again to Northampton, as overwhelmed my soul, and immediately took away my bodily strength. This was accompanied with an earnest longing, that those of us, who were the children of God, might now arise and strive. It appeared to me, that the angels in heaven sung praises for such wonderful, free, and sovereign grace, and my heart was lifted up in adoration and praise.

I continued to have clear views of the future world, of eternal happiness and misery, and my heart full of love to the souls of men. On seeing some, that were in a natural condition, I felt a most tender compassion for them; but especially was I, while I remained in the meeting house, from time to time overcome, and my bodily strength taken away, by the sight of one and another, whom I regarded as the children of God, and who, I had heard, were lively and animated in religion. We remained in the meeting house about three hours, after the public exercises were over. During most of the time, my bodily strength was overcome; and the joy and thankfulness which were excited in my mind, as I contemplated the great goodness of God, led me to converse with those who were near me, in a very earnest manner.

When I came home, I found Mr Buell, [as well as several others] at the house. Seeing and conversing with them on the Divine goodness, renewed my former feelings, and filled me with an intense desire that we might all arise, and with an active, flowing, and fervent heart give glory to God. The intenseness of my feelings took away my bodily strength. The words of one of Dr Watts' Hosannas[6] powerfully affected me, and in the course of conversation I uttered them as the real language of my heart, with great earnestness and emotion:

'Hosanna to King David's Son
Who reigns on a superior throne' ... &c.

And while I was uttering the words, my mind was so deeply impressed with the love of Christ, and a sense of his immediate presence, that I could with difficulty refrain from rising from my seat and leaping for joy. I continued to enjoy this intense, and lively, and refreshing sense of divine things, accompanied with strong emotions, for nearly an hour; after which I experienced a delightful calm, and peace, and rest in God, until I retired for the night, and during the night, both waking and sleeping, I had joyful views of divine things, and a complacential rest of soul in God.[7]

I awoke in the morning of **Thursday January 28, 1742** *in the same happy frame of mind, and engaged in the duties of my family with a sweet consciousness that God was present with me, and with earnest longings of soul for the continuance and increase of the blessed fruits of the Holy Spirit in the town.*

About 9 o clock, these desires became so exceedingly intense, when I saw numbers of the people coming into the house, with an appearance of deep interest in religion, that my bodily strength was much weakened, and it was with difficulty that I could pursue my ordinary avocations.[8]

About 11 o'clock, as I accidentally went into the room where Mr Buell was conversing with some of the people, I heard him say, 'O that we, who are the children of God, should be cold and lifeless in religion!' and I felt such a sense of the ingratitude manifested by the children of God, in such coldness and decline, that my strength was immediately taken away and I sunk down on the spot.

Those who were near raised me, and placed me in a chair, and from the fullness of my heart I expressed to them, in a very earnest manner, of the deep sense I had of the wonderful grace of God towards me, of the assurance I had of his having saved me from hell, of my happiness running parallel to eternity, of the duty of giving up all to God, and of the peace and joy inspired by an entire dependence on his mercy and grace.

Mr Buell then read a melting hymn of Dr Watt's, concerning the loveliness of Christ,[9] the enjoyments and employments of heaven, and the Christian's earnest desire of heavenly things; and the truth and reality of the things mentioned in the hymn, made such a strong impression on my mind, and my soul was drawn so powerfully towards Christ and heaven, that I leaped unconsciously from my chair.

I seemed to be drawn upwards, soul and body, from the earth towards heaven; and it appeared to me that I must naturally and necessarily ascend thither. These feelings continued while the hymn was reading, and during the prayer of Mr Christophers, which followed. After the prayer, Mr Buell read two other hymns, on the glory of heaven, which moved me so exceedingly, and drew my soul so strongly heavenwards, that it seemed, as it were, to draw my body upwards, and I felt as if I must necessarily ascend thither.

At length, my strength failed me, and I sunk down; when they took me up and laid me on my bed, where I lay for a considerable time, faint with joy, while contemplating the glories of the heavenly world. After I had lain a while, I felt more perfectly subdued and weaned from the world and more fully resigned to God than I had ever been conscious of before. I felt an entire indifference to the opinions, and representations, and conduct of mankind concerning me, and a perfect willingness that God should employ some other instrument than Mr Edwards, in advancing the work of grace in Northampton.

I was entirely swallowed up in God, as my only portion, and his honour and glory was the object of my supreme desire and delight. At the same time I felt a far greater love to the children of God, than ever before. I seemed to love them as my own soul; and when I saw them my heart went out towards them with an inexpressible endearedness and sweetness. I beheld them by faith in their risen and glorified state, with spiritual bodies re-fashioned after the image of Christ's glorious body, and arrayed in the beauty of heaven. The time when they would be so appeared very near, by faith it seemed as if it were present. This was accompanied by a ravishing sense of the unspeakable joys of the upper world. They appeared to my mind in all their reality and certainty, and as it were in actual and distinct vision; so plain and evident were they to the eye of my faith, I seemed to regard them as begun.

These anticipations were renewed over and over, while I lay on the bed, from twelve o'clock until four, being too much exhausted by emotions of joy, to rise and sit up, and during most of the time, my feelings prompted me to converse very earnestly with one and another of the pious women, who were present, on those spiritual and heavenly objects, of which I had so deep an impression.

A little while before I arose, Mr Buell and the people went to meeting. I continued in a sweet and lively sense of divine things, until I retired to rest.

*That night, which was **Thursday night January 28,** was the sweetest night I ever had in all my life. I never before, for so long a time together, enjoyed so much of the light, and rest and sweetness of heaven in my soul, but without the least agitation of body during the whole time. The great part of the night I lay awake, sometimes asleep, and sometimes between sleeping and waking. But all night I continued in a constant, clear, and lively sense of the heavenly sweetness of Christ's excellent and transcendent love, of his nearness to me, and of my dearness to him, with an inexpressibly sweet calmness of soul in an entire rest in him.*

I seemed to myself to perceive a glow of divine love come down from the heart of Christ in heaven, into my heart, in a constant stream, like a stream or pencil of sweet light. At the same time my heart and soul all flowed out in love to Christ; so that there seemed to be a constant flowing and reflowing of heavenly and divine love, from Christ's heart to mine; and I appeared to myself to float or swim, in these bright, sweet beams of the love of Christ, like the motes swimming in the beams of the sun, or the streams of his light which come in at the window.

My soul remained in a kind of heavenly elysium.[10] So far as I am capable of making a comparison, I think that what I felt each minute, during the continuance of the whole time, was worth more than all the outward comfort and pleasure which I had enjoyed in my whole life put together. It was pure delight, which fed and sustained the soul. It was pleasure, without the least sting, or any interruption. It was a sweetness, which my soul was lost in. It seemed to be all that my feeble frame could sustain, of that fullness of joy, which is felt by those who behold the face of Christ, and share in his love in the heavenly world. There was but little difference, whether I was asleep or awake, so deep was the impression made on my soul; but if there was any difference, the sweetness was greatest and most uninterrupted when I was asleep.

*As I awoke the next morning, which was **Friday January 29, 1742,** I was led to think of Mr Hadley preaching that day in the town, as had been appointed; and to examine* *my own heart, should he be extraordinarily blessed, and made a greater instrument of good in the town than Mr Edwards, and was enabled to say, with respect to that matter, 'Amen, Lord Jesus!' and be entirely willing, if God pleased, that he should be the instrument of converting every soul in town. My soul acquiesced fully in the will of God, as to the instrument, if his work of renewing grace did but go on.*

This lively sense of the beauty and excellence of divine things continued during the morning, accompanied with peculiar sweetness and delight. To my own imagination, my soul seemed to be gone out of me to God and Christ in heaven, and to have very little relation to my body.

God and Christ were so present to me, and so near me, that I seemed removed from myself. The spiritual beauty of the Father and the Saviour, seemed to engross my whole mind, and it was the instinctive feeling of my heart, 'Thou art, and there is none beside thee.'

I never felt such an entire emptiness of self-love, or any regard to any private, selfish interest of my own. It seemed to me, that I had entirely done with myself. I felt that the opinions of the world concerning me were nothing, and that I had no more to do with any outward interest of my own, than with that of a person whom I never saw. The glory of God seemed to be all, and in all, and to swallow up every wish and desire of my heart.

Mr Sheldon came into the house about 10 o'clock, and said to me as he came in, 'The Sun of righteousness arose on my soul this morning, before day' upon which I said, in reply, 'That Sun has not set upon my soul all this night; I have dwelt on high in the heavenly mansions; the light of divine love has surrounded me; my soul has been lost in God, and has almost left the body.'

This conversation only served to give me a still livelier sense of the reality and excellence of divine things, and that so such a degree, as again to take away my strength, and occasion great agitation of body.

So strong were my feelings, I could not refrain from conversing with those around me in a very earnest manner, for about a quarter of an hour, on the infinite riches of divine love in the work of salvation; when my strength entirely failing, my flesh grew very cold, and they carried me and set me by the fire. As I sat there, I had a most affecting sense of the mighty power of Christ, which had been exerted in what he had done for my soul, and in sustaining and keeping down the native corruptions of my heart, and of the glorious and wonderful grace of God in causing the ark to return to Northampton.[11]

So intense were my feelings, when speaking of these things, that I could not forbear rising and leaping with joy and exaltation. I felt at the same time an exceedingly strong and tender affection for the children of God, and realized in a manner exceedingly sweet and ravishing, the meaning of

Christ's prayer, in John 17:21: 'That they all may be one, as thou, Father, art in me, and I in thee, that they also may be one in us.'

This union appeared to me an inconceivable, excellent, and sweet oneness; and at the same time I felt that oneness in my soul, with the children of God who were present. Mr Christophers then read the hymn out of the Penitential Cries,[12] beginning with:

*'My soul doth magnify the Lord.
My spirit doth rejoice.'*

The whole hymn was deeply affecting to my feelings: but when these words were read:

*'My sighs at length are turned to songs
The Comforter has come.' –*

So conscious was I of the joyful presence of the Holy Spirit, I could scarcely refrain from leaping with transports of joy. This happy frame of mind continued until two o'clock, when Mr Williams came in, and we soon returned to meeting.

He preached on the subject of the assurance of faith. The whole sermon was affecting to me, but especially when he came to show the way in which assurance was obtained, and to point out its happy fruits. When I heard him say, that 'those who have assurance have a foretaste of heavenly glory', I knew the truth of it from what I then felt: I knew that I then tasted the clusters of the heavenly Canaan:[13] *my soul was filled and overwhelmed with light, and love, and joy in the Holy Ghost, and seemed just ready to go away from the body.*

I could scarcely refrain from expressing my joy aloud, in the midst of the service. I had, in the meantime, an overwhelming sense of the glory of God, as the Great Eternal All, and of the happiness of having my own will entirely subdued to his will.

I knew that the foretaste of glory, which I then had in my soul, came from him, that I certainly should go to him, and should, as it were, drop into the Divine Being and be swallowed up in God.

After meeting was done, the congregation waited, while Mr Buell went home, to prepare to give them a lecture. It was almost dark before he came, and, in the meantime, I conversed in a very earnest and joyful manner, with those who were with me in the pew. My mind dwelt on the thought, that the Lord God Omnipotent reigneth, and it appeared to me that he was going to set up a reign of love on the earth, and that heaven and earth were, as it were, coming together; which so exceedingly moved me, that I could not forbear expressing aloud, to those near me, my exaltation of soul.

This subsided into a heavenly calm, and a rest of soul in God, which was even sweeter than what preceded it.

*Afterwards, Mr Buell came and preached, and the same happy frame of mind continued during the evening, and night, and the next day **[Saturday January 30, 1742]**.*

In the forenoon, I was thinking of the manner in which the children of God had been treated in the world – particularly of their being shut up in prison – and the folly of such attempts to make them miserable, seemed to surprise me. It appeared astonishing that men should think by this means, to injure those who had such a kingdom within them. Towards night, being informed that Mrs P. had expressed her fears lest I should die before Mr Edwards's return, and he should think the people had killed his wife: I told those who were present, that I should be willing to die in the way that was most agreeable to God's will, and that I should be willing to die in darkness and horror, if it was most for the glory of God.

In the evening, I read those chapters in John, which contain Christ's dying discourse with his disciples, and his prayer with them. After I had done reading, and was in my retirement, a little before bedtime, thinking on what I had read, my soul was so filled with love to Christ, and love to his people, that I fainted under the intenseness of the feeling.

I felt, while reading, a delightful acquiescence in the petition to the Father – 'I pray not that thou shouldst take them out of the world, but that thou shouldst keep them from the evil.' Though it seemed to me infinitely better to die to go to Christ, yet I felt an entire willingness to continue in this world so long as God pleased, to do and suffer what he would have me.

After retiring to rest and sleeping a little while, I awoke and had a very lively consciousness of God's being near me. I had an idea of a shining way, or path of light, between heaven and my soul, somewhat as on Thursday night, except that God seemed nearer to me, and as it were, close by me, and the way seemed more open, and the communication more immediate and more free.

*I lay awake most of the night, with a constant delightful sense of God's great love and infinite condescension, and with a continual view of God as **near** and as **my God**. My soul remained, as on Thursday night, in a kind of heavenly elysium. Whether waking or sleeping, there was no interruption, throughout the night, to the views of my soul, to its heavenly light and divine, inexpressible sweetness. It was without any agitation or motion of the body. I was led to reflect on God's mercy to me, in giving me, for so many years, a willingness to die; and after that, for more than two years past, in making me willing to live, that I might do and suffer whatever he called me to here; whereas, before that, I often used to feel impatient at the thought of living.*

This then appeared to me as it had often done before, what gave me much the greatest sense of thankfulness to God. I also thought how God had graciously given me, for a great while, an entire resignation to his will, with respect to the kind and manner of death that I should die; having been made willing to die on the rack, or at the stake, or any other kind of tormenting death, and, if it were God's will to die in darkness: and how I had that day been made very sensible and fully willing, if it were God's pleasure and for his glory, to die in horror.

But now it occurred to me, that when I had thus been made willing to live, and to be kept on this dark abode, I used to think of living no longer than to the ordinary age of man. Upon this, I was led to ask myself, Whether I was not willing to be kept out of heaven even longer; and my whole heart seemed immediately to reply, 'Yes, a thousand times, if it be God's will, and for his honour and glory': and then, my heart, in the language of resignation went further, and with great alacrity and sweetness, to answer as it were, over and over again, 'Yes, and live a thousand years in horror, if it be most for the glory of God: yea, I was willing to live a thousand years a hell upon earth, if it be most for the honour of God.' But then I considered with myself, What this would be, to live a hell upon earth, for so long a time: and I thought of the torment of my body being so great, awful, and overwhelming that, that none could bear to live in the country where the spectacle was seen, and of the torment and horror of my mind being vastly greater than the torment of my body, and it seemed to me that I found a perfect willingness and sweet quietness and alacrity[14] *of soul, in consenting that it should be so, if it were most for the glory of God: so that there was no hesitation, doubt or darkness in my mind, attending the thoughts of it, but my resignation seemed to be clear, like a light that shone through my soul.*

I continued saying, 'Amen, Lord Jesus! Amen, Lord Jesus! Glorify thyself in me, in my body and my soul' – with a calm and sweetness of soul, which banished all reluctance. The glory of God seemed to overcome me and swallow me up, and every conceivable suffering, and everything that was terrible to my nature, seemed to shrink to nothing before it.

This resignation continued in its clearness and brightness the rest of the night, and all the next day, and the night following, and on Monday in the forenoon, without interruption or abatement. All this while, whenever I thought of it, the language of my soul was, with the greatest fullness and alacrity, 'Amen, Lord Jesus! Amen, Lord Jesus!'

*In the afternoon of **Monday [February 1]**, it was not quite so perceptible and lively, but my mind remained so much in a similar frame, for more than a week **[ie February 1–8]**, that I could never think of it without an inexpressible sweetness in my soul.*

*After I had felt this resignation on **Saturday night [February 6]**, for some time as I lay in bed, I felt such a disposition to rejoice in God, that I wished to have the world join me in praising him; and was ready to wonder how the world of mankind could lie and sleep, when there* *was such a God to praise, and rejoice in, and could scarcely forbear calling out to those who were asleep in the house, to arise, and rejoice, and praise God.*

*When I arose on the morning of the **Sabbath [February 7]**, I felt a love to all mankind, wholly peculiar in its strength and sweetness, far beyond all that I had ever felt before. The power of that love seemed to be inexpressible. I thought, if I were surrounded by enemies, who were venting their malice and cruelty upon me, in tormenting me, it would still be impossible that I should cherish any feelings towards them but those of love and pity, and ardent desire for their holiness. At the same time, I thought, if I were cast off by my nearest and dearest friends, and if the feelings and conduct of my husband were to be changed from tenderness and affection, to extreme hatred and cruelty, and that every day, I could so rest in God, that it would not touch my heart, or diminish my happiness. I could still go on with alacrity in the performance of every act of duty, and my happiness remain undiminished and entire.*

I never before felt so far from a disposition to judge and censure others, with respect to the state of their own hearts, their sincerity, or their attainments in holiness, as I did that morning. To do this seemed abhorrent to every feeling of my heart. I realised also, in an unusual and very lively manner, how great a part of Christianity lies in the performance of social and relative duties to one another.

Testimony: 'My God, my all'

The same lively and joyful sense of spiritual and divine things continued throughout the day – a sweet love to God and all mankind, and such an entire rest of soul in God, that it seemed as if nothing that could be said of me, or done to me, could touch my heart, or disturb my enjoyment.

The road between heaven and my soul seemed open and wide, all the day long; and the consciousness I had of the reality and excellence of heavenly things was so clear, and the affections they excited so intense, that it overcame my strength, and kept my body weak and faint, the great part of the day, so that I could neither stand nor go without help. The night also was comforting and refreshing.

*This delightful frame of mind was continued on **Monday [February 8]**. About noon, one of the neighbours who was conversing with me, expressed himself thus, 'One smile from Christ is worth a thousand million pounds', and the words affected me exceedingly, and in a manner which I cannot express. I had a strong sense of the infinite worth of Christ's approbation and love, and at the same time of the grossness of the comparison; and it only astonished me that anyone could compare a smile of Christ to any earthly treasure.*

Towards night, I had a deep sense of the awful greatness of God, and felt with what humility and reverence we ought to behave ourselves towards him. Just then, Mr W. came in and spoke with a somewhat light, smiling air of the flourishing state of religion in the town, which I could scarcely bear to see. It seemed to me, that we ought greatly to revere the presence of God, and to behave ourselves with the utmost solemnity and humility, when so great and holy a God was so remarkably present, and to rejoice before him with trembling.

In the evening, these words in the Penitential Cries 'The Comforter is come!'[15] were accompanied to my soul with such conscious certainty, and such intense joy, that immediately it took away my strength, and I was falling to the floor; when some of those who were near me caught me and held me up.

And when I repeated the words to bystanders, the strength of my feelings was increased. The name, 'THE COMFORTER', seemed to denote that the Holy Spirit was the only and infinite Fountain of comfort and joy, and this seemed real and certain to my mind. These words – 'THE COMFORTER' – seemed as it were immensely great, enough to fill heaven and earth.

*On **Tuesday [February 9]** after dinner, Mr Buell, as he sat at table, began to discourse about the glories of the upper world, which greatly affected me, so as to take away my strength. The views, and feelings of the preceding evening, respecting the Great Comforter, were renewed in the most lively and joyful manner; so that my limbs grew cold, and I continued, to a considerable degree overcome for about an hour, earnestly expressing to those around me, my deep* *and joyful sense of the presence and divine excellencies of the Comforter, and of the glories of heaven.*

*It was either on **Tuesday or Wednesday [February 9/10]**, that Mr W. came to the house, and informed what account Mr Lyman, who was just then come from Leicester, on his way from Boston, gave of Mr Edwards's success in making peace and promoting religion at Leicester.*

The intelligence inspired me with such an admiring sense of the great goodness of God in using Mr Edwards as the instrument of doing good, and promoting the work of salvation, that it immediately overcame me, and took away my strength, so that I could no longer stand on my feet.

*On **Wednesday night [February 10]**, Mr Clark, coming in with Mr Buell and some of the people, asked me how I felt. I told him that I did not feel at all times alike, but this I thought I could say, that I had given up all to God; and there is nothing like it, nothing like giving up all to him, esteeming all to be his, and resigning all to his will. I told him that many a time within a twelve-month, I had asked myself when I lay down, How I should feel, if our house, and all our property should be burned up, and if we should that night be turned out naked; whether I could cheerfully resign all to God, and whether I so saw that all was his, that I could fully consent to his will, in being deprived of it? and that I found, so far as I could judge, an entire resignation to his will, and felt that, if he should thus strip me of everything, I had nothing to say, but should, I* *thought, have an entire rest and calm in God, for it was his own, and not mine.*

After that, Mr Phelps gave me an account of his own feelings, during a journey from which he had just returned; and then Mr Pomeroy broke forth in the language of joy, and thankfulness, and praise, and continued speaking to us nearly an hour, leading us all the time to rejoice in the visible presence of God and to adore his infinite goodness and condescension.

He concluded by saying, 'I would say more if I could; but words were not made to express these things. This reminded me of the words of Mrs Rowe:[16]

'More I would speak, but all my words are faint: Celestial Love, what eloquence can paint? No more, by mortal words can be expressed: But vast Eternity shall tell the rest.'

and my former impressions of heavenly and divine things were renewed with so much power, and life, and joy, that my strength all failed me, and I remained for some time faint and exhausted.

After the people had retired, I had a still more lively and joyful sense of the goodness and all sufficiency of God, of the pleasure of loving him, and of being alive and active in his service, so that I could not sit still, but walked in the room for some time, in a kind of transport.

The contemplation was so refreshing and delightful, so much like a heavenly feast within the soul, that I felt an absolute indifference to any external circumstances; and according to my best remembrance, this enlivening of my spirit continued, so that I slept but little that night.

*The next day, being **Thursday [February 11]**, between two and eleven o'clock, and a room full of people being collected, I heard two persons give a minute account of the enlivening and joyful influences of the Holy Spirit on their own hearts. It was sweet to me to see others before me in their divine attainments, and to follow after them to heaven. I thought I should rejoice to follow the servants in the town to heaven. While I was thus listening, the consideration of the blessed appearances there were of God's being there with us, affected me so powerfully, that the joy and transport of the preceding night were again renewed.*

After this, they sang a hymn, which greatly moved me, especially the latter part of it which speaks of the ungratefulness of not having the praise of Christ always on our tongues. Those last words of the hymn seemed to fasten on my mind, and as I repeated them over, I felt such an intense love to Christ, and so much delight in praising him, that I could hardly forbear leaping from my chair, and singing aloud for joy and exaltation. I continued thus extraordinarily moved until about one o'clock, when the people went away.

Having set down his wife's account of her experience, Jonathan Edwards acknowledged that it would make no sense to anyone who did not know God for themselves:

> *Those who have no concept of what is meant by the religion of the heart, will dismiss it as the result of physical or mental illness. Others will dismiss it as mere enthusiasm.*[17]

For him, the test of the reality of his wife's experience was her life. He observed the way that she consistently enjoyed fellowship with the Triune God, Father, Son and Holy Spirit. He observed how, both before and after this time, she longed for God's glory, and put the interests of others ahead of her own. After this experience she was more humble, more aware of her own short-comings, more reluctant to judge others, and liberated from anxiety in situations of pain or uncertainty. She lived a life of service to God and others 'doing it as the service of love with uninterrupted cheerfulness, peace and joy'.[18]

> *Instead of neglecting the business of life, she performed it with greater alacrity as a part of her service to God, declaring that when it was thus done, it was as delightful as prayer itself. At the same time, she discovered an extreme anxiety to avoid every sin, and to discharge every moral obligation, was most exemplary in the performance of every social and relative duty, exhibited great inoffensiveness of life and conversation, great meekness, gentleness, and benevolence of spirit, and avoided, with remarkable conscientiousness, all those things which she regarded as failings in her own character.*[19]

He concluded:

> *Now if such things are enthusiasm, and the offspring of a distempered brain, let my brain be possessed for evermore of that happy distemper!*[20] *If this be distraction; I pray God that the world of mankind may all be seized with this benign, meek, beatific, glorious distraction!*[21]

He argued that there were widespread, lasting and beneficial effects from the revival, concluding:

> *This work, which has lately been carried on in the land, is a work of God, and not the work of men.*[22]

During those weeks Sarah had experienced God's love in a way that is best described as a foretaste of heaven. Such intensity of experience cannot be sustained for lengthy periods.[23] And such intense experiences are characteristic of unusual times of revival. God is sovereign, and works in different times and different ways. At a few points during this time Sarah was laid low physically, and unable to do her normal day to day duties. There were moments when some parishioners wondered whether she would even survive. But they didn't question the reality of her spiritual experience. Her account indicates that the parsonage was full of many people over these weeks, so we can infer that the needs of the family and guests continued to be met by both household servants and parishioners. Over the long term this profound experience better equipped her for her ongoing ministries in her family and community.

The so-called Great Awakening of the eighteenth century transformed the Protestant church, and laid the foundations for the modern mission movement. The revival took hold of peoples' emotions. Truth seemed to come alive. 'I **feel** my Saviour in my heart,' wrote Charles Wesley.[24] As in any religious movement there were aberrations and excesses, but Jonathan believed that Sarah's intense experience represented the purest elements in that revival period. It was based on biblical truth, not divorced from it. Most importantly, it would stand the test of suffering in the following years.

Questions for reflection

1. Which aspects of Sarah Edwards' religious experience do you want to characterise your own relationship with the Lord?

2. How should this affect your priorities in prayer for yourself and others?

PART 3

Depending on God

When I remember you upon my bed,
and meditate on you in the watches of the night;
for you have been my help,
and in the shadow of your wings I will sing for joy.
My soul clings to you;
your right hand upholds me.

Psalm 63:6–8

7

Testing: 'A resignation of all to God'

The reality of Sarah's 'resignation of all to God' would be tested all too soon.

While carried away with a sense of the love of God, she had visualised a series of worst-case scenarios. What if the townsfolk turned on her and she was thrown out into the wilderness during winter? What if her husband turned against her? What if she had to die for Christ? More to the point, what about living the difficult day-to-day routine uncomplainingly? She was only 32, and having already had seven children, there were four more confinements ahead with all the pain, danger and exhaustion that involved. By December of 1742 she was pregnant with her eighth child, and needed medical attention.[1]

But soon Sarah was facing situations she had not imagined: war, slander, bereavement, poverty, a move to an isolated frontier settlement and, finally, the loss of her beloved husband. Her professed security in the love of God would be tested to the limit.

War

England and France went to war in 1744. Inhabitants of towns such as Northampton were the targets of attack, because French Canadians were paying their allies among the North American Indians to kill English settlers. Gruesome killings took place daily. Both sides paid bounties for enemy scalps. The Edwards' garden was chosen as the site of a watchtower in 1745, from which the Northampton militia stood guard against attack. At this point, baby Eunice was two years old, and little Jonathan just a newborn. Several in Northampton were killed. The town was on high alert. In 1746, the Edwards sent two of their daughters, Sarah (18) and Esther (14), down to Long Island to stay with friends for safety. Jonathan wrote to them:

> Our house is now forted [fortified] in, and a watch is kept here every night in the fort ... your circumstances are on some accounts more comfortable than those of your sisters at home, for you lie down and arise and have none to make you afraid. Here we have been much in fear of an army suddenly rushing in upon the town in the night to destroy it.[2]

This was not just a local struggle – it was part of a global conflict between two great naval powers. Many feared that victory for the French Catholic side would usher in a grim era of persecution of Protestants.[3] More immediately, war brought fear, insecurity, financial chaos, the devaluing of currency and great economic hardship. The parishioners found it hard to feed their own families, and they were not always able – or willing – to hand over tithes for the Edwards' upkeep. Jonathan and Sarah were in the embarrassing situation of having to remind the parish to pay their salary. Jonathan (like other ministers of the time) felt the need to get his salary arranged on a more regular basis. This did not go down well with his parishioners. Sarah faced the indignity of having to submit detailed and itemised accounts of all family expenditures. The townsfolk wanted proof that the Edwards were not guilty of extravagance.

Slander and intrigue

The dispute over salary was symptomatic of the widening breach between Jonathan and the Northampton church. Relationships degenerated after the end of revival in 1742. A party came together who were determined to get rid of Jonathan – including some of his own relatives.

The Edwards did have faithful friends. Chief among them was Jonathan's uncle, Colonel Stoddard, a pillar of the community, whose strong personality and reputation shielded them from some of the opposition. But Colonel Stoddard fell critically ill during a visit to New York in 1748. He asked Sarah to come down to nurse him in his final sickness. She left her baby with a neighbour's wife and went.[4] His death left the family more vulnerable.

Jonathan's ministry had seemed so successful during the years of growth from 1734 to 1742. Why this opposition?

Social and religious forces bigger than the local situation were at work. Revival had unleashed forces of individualism that were profoundly anti-authority. Church members were willing to question their pastor's judgement, and if he did not agree with them, why not dismiss him? They too had experienced the Holy Spirit!

The eighteenth century also saw a 'levelling' in American society. The old assumption that the minister, as a member of the gentry class, was entitled to a higher standard of living than the bulk of his parishioners came under attack. The Edwards were caught in the backlash. There may have been a culture gap between the Edwards (who were well educated and used to life in a larger town) and their farming neighbours.

As the eighteenth century progressed, the ideal of the community being identified with the church became outdated. Was the minister really to consider himself responsible for the morality of the town? In 1744, some of the young adults in the town were found joking over the illustrations in a midwifery handbook. A tragi-comic spectacle unfolded. From the pulpit, Jonathan read out the names of all those involved, whether participants or witnesses. This was a huge mistake. All were shamed and angry, and they represented every important family in the town.

The most significant cause of disagreement was a dispute over who should take communion. Solomon Stoddard, Jonathan's grandfather had not required a profession of saving faith before church members could take communion.[5] This was a sensitive issue, as only communicant members of the church could hold civic office in the town. By 1744, Jonathan had become convinced that only those who professed conversion should be admitted to church membership and allowed to take communion.

He could not carry the church with him on this issue. They thought he was desecrating the memory of his revered grandfather. He was also challenging the cherished privileges of townsfolk. This issue stirred up tensions between 'nominal' church members, including some of Edwards' wider family, and the others.

In 1747, Joseph Hawley Jr was elected to civic office in Northampton. He was young, dynamic, gifted, eloquent – and the ringleader of opposition to Jonathan. (He would later confess that he had circulated slanders in his effort to get his cousin dismissed.)

In the following year, as the death of Colonel Stoddard removed one of Jonathan's most loyal supporters, the weight of influence in the extended family tipped over to Israel Williams, another cousin of Jonathan, who had opposed him since 1734.

Jonathan's stand on the communion question provoked a furore, not only in Northampton, but in the surrounding area. Ill-feeling was stirred up and misrepresentations circulated. Sarah felt compelled to take up her pen in her husband's defence. She described the way he had genuinely changed his mind over the years. Here are some extracts from her (much longer) letter:

> *I do testify and declare that above four years ago, not very long after Mr. Edwards had admitted the last Person that ever was admitted into this church who made no Profession of Godliness, He told me that He would not dare ever to*

*admit another Person without a Profession of real saving
Religion; and the same Time told me he had put something
into his Book on Religious Affections by which the Country
would know his opinion, and that He had done it on
Design that They might have some Intimation of it …
He often touched on this matter in discourse with me …
and often signified that when He should begin to have
Occasion to act on his Principles, or when any offered to
come into the Church, that made no pretence to Godliness,
& He should be obliged to refuse, then the Tumult would
begin … I remember Mr. Edwards once in talking to some
Gentleman of these matters Expressed Himself thus, that
the difficulties He had a Prospect of appeared to Him like a
Bottomless ocean, He could see no end of 'em.*[6]

The church dismissed Jonathan in June 1750, leaving the
family with no financial support. Jonathan preached his farewell sermon on 1 July 1750. He reminded his congregation
that they would all meet before God at the Last Judgement,
and they would all give account to him:

*We must meet one another before the chief Shepherd – when
I must give an account of my stewardship, of the service
I have done, and the reception and treatment I have had
among the people to whom He sent me. And you must
give an account of your own conduct towards me and the
improvement you have made of these three and twenty
years of my ministry. For then both you and I must appear
together, and we both must give an account, in order to an
infallible righteous and eternal sentence to be passed upon*

us, by Him Who will judge us with respect to all that we
have said or done in our meetings here, all our conduct one
towards another, in the house of God and elsewhere.[7]

Jonathan continued to write. He corresponded with friends in
Scotland (and elsewhere) on profound theological issues. His
concerns extended far beyond what was going on in his own
parish. But day-to-day life was difficult. The scenario enacted
in Sarah's imagination during her revival experience in
essence, if not in exact detail, had come to pass – although to
be physically thrown out of the town might have been easier
than the long months of living among unfriendly faces. The
family did not move away from Northampton for a year and
four months after the dismissal. During that time, they continued to attend the church, and Jonathan was willing to supply
the pulpit when called on. But the hostility against Edwards
and his family from within the community was deeply hurtful.

There could have been no more effective test of Sarah's
profession of love and humility. In the early days of 1742,
while overwhelmed with awareness of God's love, she had
been filled with intense love towards others. She could not
imagine bearing ill-will towards another person. Now, in the
aftermath of the dismissal, it was evident that her experience
had been genuine. Jonathan and Sarah were free of resent-
ment or bitterness. They were shut up to the opinion of all
but God. In 1754, Joseph Hawley wrote to them, apologising
for his part in opposing them. After Jonathan and Sarah's
death, he published a public letter of apology for the mali-
cious slanders that had been circulated.

Bereavement

Sarah had felt able to submit whether she lived or died to God. It is often more difficult for a mother to submit the lives of her children. Sarah now experienced this trial for the first time.

In early 1747, David Brainerd, a young missionary to the North American Indians, arrived at the Edwards' home. He was suffering from tuberculosis. Sarah, aged 37, was pregnant with her tenth child, so Jerusha volunteered to nurse their dying guest. At that time, it was not realised that tuberculosis (consumption) is infectious. David died in October 1747; 17-year-old Jerusha had contracted the illness from him and died in the following February.

Jonathan wrote to a Scottish friend that she had been 'the flower of the family'. He preached her funeral sermon from Job 14:2, reminding his hearers that even young people may be like flowers that are cut down. That was a 'fit emblem of a young person in the bloom of life,' he said: Jerusha had been beautiful in body, mind and soul. She had been 'indifferent about all things whatsoever of a worldly nature, setting her heart' on another world.[8]

The Sunday before her death, Jerusha had attended church, with no sign of what was to happen the next week. The family was comforted to know that she was with Christ. This providence was bitter. But perhaps it would warn other young people. What if they were suddenly to be cut off in the bloom of life? What would happen to them?

The text chosen for Jerusha's grave was Psalm 17:15: 'I shall be satisfied, when I awake, with thy likeness.'

This tragedy hit the family hard. Three months later, Sarah gave birth to her only unhealthy baby. Little Elizabeth suffered from rickets and was pitifully frail. Six years later, Sarah's daughter Esther wrote to her best friend Sarah Prince: 'We shall never forget the friends we have lost by death. I mean our Sisters.'[9]

Poverty

When Jonathan was dismissed from Northampton, his salary stopped. He had a wife and children to provide for. Bills still had to be paid, and lack of income soon began to bite. Friends in Scotland took up a generous collection for them, but it took time to arrive in New England. The strain told on Sarah – she went down with rheumatic fever. She had been brought up in wealth and comfort, but she was willing to work hard. She had trained her daughters in the art of needlework and fine embroidery, and they set to work to help the family finances. They also engaged in every possible economy. Scraps of paper were retrieved and sewn together, and Jonathan wrote some of the greatest treatises ever produced in church history on these patchwork pieces of paper.

Two months before the dismissal, Sarah gave birth to a son, their last child, who was given her maiden name, Pierpont. Just two weeks before Jonathan was dismissed, her oldest child Sarah, aged 21, married a faithful and loyal townsman, Elihu Parsons. Another wedding took place in November 1750: their fourth daughter, 16-year-old Mary, married Timothy Dwight, their neighbour in Northampton. These were all welcome causes of thanksgiving at such a difficult time.

In October 1751, the family moved to Stockbridge, a missionary settlement on the frontier, about 60 miles from

Northampton. Here Jonathan Edwards would minister to around 200 Mahican Indians,[10] a smaller number of Mohawks, and a handful of English families.[11]

Life on the frontier

Now 42, Sarah had the task of settling her large family into a new situation. The natural beauty surrounding them was stunning, and winter provided wonderful opportunities sledging and skating – much appreciated by Esther (20), Lucy (15), Timothy (13), Susanna (11), Eunice (8) and Jonathan Jr (6). Young Jonathan made firm friends with numerous Indian children and soon became bilingual. Little Elizabeth (4) was fragile, and would have to spend much time indoors, along with baby Pierpont. Sarah herself became dangerously ill in the October of 1752.[12]

Even in that small settlement, tensions abounded. Two leading English families (related to the Edwards) saw it as their mission to continue the Northampton opposition. But Jonathan set about his duties with characteristic resolve. He preached (via an interpreter) to both groups of Indians, as well as to the tiny English congregation. He continued to write. Friendships were maintained. Sarah gave hospitality to friends who travelled to see them. Their close friend Samuel Hopkins lived seven miles away and they always enjoyed his visits.

In the summer of 1752, Sarah had the joy of seeing their third daughter happily married. Aaron Burr, the 36-year-old president of New Jersey College, travelled north to Stockbridge in order to propose to Esther. She had no hesitation in accepting, despite the 17-year age gap. The wedding took place down in New Jersey. Sarah travelled with Esther for the marriage. Shortly afterwards, 14-year-old Timothy was sent down to study at New Jersey College (then located at Newark).

Then there was the arrival of grandchildren. Their oldest daughter Sarah's first baby died – she needed her family's support, so she and her husband moved from Northampton up to Stockbridge. After that they had healthy children, as did Mary and Esther. Sarah tried, when possible, to be at the birth of her grandchildren. At that time, family members commonly acted as midwives. When Esther had her first child in the spring of 1754, Sarah travelled down to New Jersey to be with her.

Increased tensions on the wider front as well as within the settlement took their toll. Jonathan was seriously ill for seven months between July 1754 and February 1755. The community was facing renewed threats from French-supported Huron Indians. In September, Hurons broke into the settlement and killed and scalped three members of one English family. A fort was built around the Edwards' home. During the construction, Sarah cooked 180 meals for the builders, in addition to 800 meals for refugees fleeing the interior. When soldiers were sent to Stockbridge, Sarah was expected to feed them, but her budget could not stretch that far. Jonathan wrote to the officer in charge to say that they could not afford to supply more than four soldiers with provisions.

Friends and family begged the Edwards to leave Stockbridge, even temporarily, as they were dangerously exposed to attack. Jonathan and Sarah believed they were safer in the path of duty than out of it and stayed, although they sent some of the children down to Northampton, further away from danger.

Esther paid a surprise visit to her parents in September 1756, but couldn't sleep for fear while staying in Stockbridge. Her visit was all the more miserable because a few days after her arrival, Sarah left to go back to Northampton to support Mary during childbirth. It cannot have been easy for Sarah to leave Esther and her new grandchild Aaron, for she did not know when she would be able to see them again. But Mary needed her more.

Jonathan continued to minister to the Indians in the immediate vicinity. He had a high regard for them, and the respect was mutual. 'The Indians seem much pleased with my family, especially my wife,' he wrote.[13] Jonathan invested much energy in promoting education. He was shocked that the Indians had so often been exploited, and he did not condone many of the English policies towards the Indians.[14]

Jonathan's hope that his son Jonathan would eventually minister to the Indians would, in time, be fulfilled. At age 9, young Jonathan was already fluent in one Indian language. He was then sent to live with an English missionary for two years to learn another (based 200 miles away near the Susquehanna River). In time, he became a theologian, a pioneer in the historical linguistics of Native North America, and a firm opponent of slavery.

Questions for reflection

1. In what ways did Sarah Edwards prove the reality of her faith and changed life?

2. Think back to times when you have been able to find strength in God's promises, and give thanks to God for his faithfulness.

8

Death:
'My God lives, and he has my heart'

After just five years of marriage, Esther's husband, Aaron Burr, died of a fever, aged only 41.[1] This proved to be the catalyst for further tragedies. Jonathan, now aged 54, was invited to take Burr's place as President of the New Jersey College (by then located at Princeton).[2] He was reluctant to move, as he was now in a situation where he could focus on his many writing projects. But he placed the decision in the hands of a council of ministers, and they advised that he should accept the post. Jonathan wept when he heard this, but accepted it as God's will – and as his duty. He moved down to Princeton in January 1758 to be with his widowed daughter. Sarah was left in Stockbridge to finish packing their belongings, and the family planned to join Jonathan later in the spring.

Jonathan moved into the President's house in Princeton, along with Esther and her two children Sally (4) and Aaron (2). Soon after arriving, Jonathan heard that his father, Timothy Edwards, had died on 27 January, aged 89. His mother, Esther Edwards (née Stoddard) would live on until she was 98. She was well known for her deep godliness; many women would gather in her home to hear her speak and pray. She was a voracious reader, well able to share what she had learned from the best theological writings.[3]

By the February of 1758, many in the Princeton area had fallen ill with smallpox. This was one of the scourges of the era – at one point it caused a tenth of all deaths in Europe. Through the eighteenth century, inoculation became more commonplace.[4] Jonathan, Esther and the two children were all inoculated. Esther and the children recovered well, but Jonathan became critically ill. On his deathbed, he sent word to his wife, thanking God for the 'uncommon union' that they had enjoyed and would enjoy for eternity. He died on 22 March 1758. His last words were: 'Trust in God and you need not fear.'[5]

When Sarah received the news, she was suffering a painful illness herself. Amid the pain, she had been preparing to travel to support her newly widowed mother-in-law. But she responded to this next tragedy with faith and courage. As Sereno Edwards Dwight noted:

> *She had long told her intimate friends, that she had, after long struggles and exercises, obtained by God's grace a habitual willingness to die herself, or part with any of her most near relatives ... and to resign her nearest partner, to*

the stroke of death, whenever God should see fit to take him. And when she had the greatest trial, in the death of Mr Edwards, she found the help and comfort of such a disposition ... she was sensible of the great loss, which she and her children had sustained in his death, and yet at the same time, showed that she was quiet and resigned and had those invisible supports, which enabled her to trust in God with quietness, hope and humble joy.[6]

Sarah managed to write a brief and heartfelt note to Esther:

Stockbridge, April 3rd, 1758.

My very dear child,

What shall I say? A holy and good God has covered us with a dark cloud. O that we may kiss the rod and lay our hands on our mouths! The Lord has done it. He has made me adore his goodness that we had him [her husband] so long. But my God lives; and he has my heart. O what a legacy my husband and your father has left us! We are all given to God; and there I am, and love to be.

Your ever affectionate mother, Sarah Edwards.[7]

Esther never received this letter. She died, aged 26, only 16 days after her father's death, leaving two little children.

Sarah then left her own children – Pierpont aged only 8 – and travelled a hundred miles down to New Jersey to collect the two orphaned grandchildren. Despite arriving in good health, she soon contracted dysentery, and became critically ill during her homeward journey. She died on 2 October 1758, aged just 48:

> *She apprehended her death was near, then she expressed her entire resignation to go, and her desire that He might be glorified in all things, and that she might be enabled to glorify Him to the last; and [she] continued in such a temper, calm and resigned, till she died.*[8]

Throughout her life, and during the final tragic series of events, and in her last hours, Sarah could testify:

> *For I am persuaded that neither death nor life, nor angels nor principalities nor powers, nor things present nor things to come, nor height nor depth, nor any other created thing shall be able to separate us from the love of God which is in Christ Jesus our Lord. (Romans 8:38–39, NKJV)*

Questions for reflection

1. Before her husband died, Sarah Edwards testified that for many years she had surrendered her loved ones (and her own life) to God. Reflect on how this equipped her to face bereavement and death with peace.

2. Sarah could testify that 'nothing could separate' her from God's love. To what extent do you know that type of assurance?

9

Legacy: Desiring God's glory

From an early age, Sarah Edwards had delighted in God. Her enduring delight in God through the final years of suffering was based on the conviction that God is sovereign in history. She trusted his wisdom and his goodness – and was confident that nothing happens outside of his control. Far from being self-absorbed, she took comfort in the wider perspective. God's supreme goal is the glory of his Son. Christ seeks the glory of his Father (1 Corinthians 15:24). The ultimate success of that goal was secured at the Cross.

The Edwards' concerns extended far beyond personal, family or parochial affairs *because* they were certain of the cosmic triumph of Christ. That conviction was laid out in a sermon Jonathan preached from 1 Corinthians 15:25–26: 'For he must reign until he has put all his enemies under his feet. The last enemy to be destroyed is death.'[1]

He began with a graphic overview of the many evils in the world, including death itself. The main part of the sermon described how Christ has triumphed over each one of them. All the hideous expressions of evil in history were, are and will be the occasion for Christ's glory to be exalted. New manifestations of evil will arise until Christ's return, but we are not to give way to sinful discouragement.

The year after that sermon was preached, Jonathan preached a series of 30 sermons on the theme of *The History of Redemption* based around two verses from Isaiah 51:[2]

Fear not the reproach of man,
nor be dismayed at their revilings.
For the moth will eat them up like a garment,
and the worm will eat them like wool,
but my righteousness will be forever,
and my salvation to all generations. (Isaiah 51:7–8)

One 10-year-old boy in the congregation[3] later recalled being transfixed as Edwards laid out a stunning overview of history from Creation to the Second Coming.[4] History is not just a random series of events. It is the history of Redemption. It is the overflow in time of the eternal inter-trinitarian love of God. It is the 'language of God's redemptive love'.[5] There is a cosmic conflict going on between God's kingdom, and the forces of darkness, but victory was won at Calvary. The little stone which smashes ungodly empires is filling and will fill the whole earth.[6]

That eternal and global perspective enabled Sarah to remain God-centred, even when facing war, poverty, slander sickness and bereavement. She was convinced that God is

worthy of the praise of every person on earth, and she could
not bear to think of him not receiving his due.

> *I felt such a disposition to rejoice in God, that I wished*
> *to have the world join me in praising him. I was ready to*
> *wonder how the world of mankind could lie and sleep when*
> *there was such a God to praise![7]*

As we read about Jonathan and Sarah Edwards, surely we
should pray that 'something of their fire will kindle in our
soul'.[8] But the account of Sarah's extraordinary experience
may leave readers with the question: Is such an experience
something we should all be seeking?

Throughout Scripture we are encouraged to pray for a
deeper knowledge of God. The apostle Paul prayed:

> *... that you, being rooted and grounded in love, may have*
> *strength to comprehend with all the saints what is the*
> *breadth and length and height and depth, and to know the*
> *love of Christ that surpasses knowledge, that you may be*
> *filled with all the fullness of God. (Ephesians 3:17–19)*

Paul himself testified of a time when he had an experience of
God's love so intense, that it was as if he had been caught up
to heaven (2 Corinthians 12:2). But it was followed by times
of severe trial (2 Corinthians 12:7–10).

Many Christians can speak of the extremity of the contrast
between times when God is felt to be very near, and times
when he seems far away. One of the most evocative portrayals
of that contrast is found in a poem by George Herbert:

How should I praise thee, Lord! How should my rhymes
Gladly engrave thy love in steel,
If what my soul doth feel sometimes,
My soul might ever feel!

Although there were some forty heav'ns, or more,
Sometimes I peer above them all;
Sometimes I hardly reach a score;
Sometimes to hell I fall.

O rack me not to such a vast extent;
Those distances belong to thee:
The world's too little for thy tent,
A grave too big for me.

Yet take thy way; for sure thy way is best:
Stretch or contract me thy poor debtor:
This is but tuning of my breast,
To make the music better.

Whether I fly with angels, fall with dust,
Thy hands made both, and I am there;
Thy power and love, my love and trust,
Make one place ev'rywhere.[9]

'Thy power and love, my love and trust, make one place ev'rywhere': the essence of faith is persevering through the dark times because God is with us!

God is sovereign. He works at different times, in different ways. He may not necessarily work in us in the same way as he has done with other believers. But we are encouraged in Scripture to pray and work for God's will to be done and for his name to be honoured – in our own lives and then more widely. Jonathan and Sarah Edwards were always eager to hear of the progress of God's kingdom in other countries. Today we have a far greater access to knowledge of how the church is expanding in every nation. We can use those resources to pray for and work for the extension of God's kingdom.

As we reflect on the extent of the unfinished task, we should pray that 'the word of the Lord may speed ahead and be honoured' (2 Thessalonians 3:1). In *A History of the Work of Redemption,* Jonathan Edwards presented evidence to show that revivals of religion are a key way in which God's kingdom is extended.[10] They are times when 'God draws near', when eternal realities are vividly sensed, and when gospel work progresses rapidly. Jonathan and Sarah were part of an international community of Christians who united in prayer that the gospel would go out to all nations, and who promoted and prayed for revival.

One of the case studies of revival cited in *History of Redemption* was the account of Auguste Hermann Francke (1663–1727), a European leader of church renewal. Franke's personal mission statement was: 'A life changed, a church revived, a nation reformed, and a world evangelised.'[11]

That sums up the priorities of Sarah and Jonathan Edwards. It should be our desire too.

Questions for reflection

1. Sarah Edwards' enduring delight in God through the final years of suffering was based on the conviction

that God is sovereign in history. How does that truth encourage you?

2. Can you say (with the prophet Isaiah): 'Yes, Lord, walking in the way of your laws, we wait for you; *your name and renown are the desire of our hearts*' (Isaiah 26:8)?

Further resources

The best starting point for a biography of Jonathan and Sarah Edwards is:
Iain H. Murray, *Jonathan Edwards: A New Biography*, Banner of Truth Trust, 1987.

Other resources

Jennifer Adams, ed, *In Love with Christ: The Narrative of Sarah Edwards*, Corner Pillar Press, 2015.

Elisabeth D. Dodds, *Marriage to a Difficult Man: The 'Uncommon Union' of Jonathan and Sarah Edwards*, Westminster Press, 1975.

Edna Gerstner, *Jonathan and Sarah: An Uncommon Union*, Soli Deo Gloria Publications, 1995. A semi-fictional account.

Michael A. G. Haykin, *Eight Women of Faith*, Crossway, 2016. Includes chapters on Sarah Edwards and her daughter, Esther Burr.

Michael A. G. Haykin, 'A Sin of the First Magnitude: Samuel Hopkins and American Slavery' (unpublished paper).

Irene Howatt, *10 Girls Who Used Their Talents for God*, Christian Focus, 2014. Includes a section on Sarah Edwards, for girls, 7–12 years old.

Carol F. Karlsen and Laurie Crumpacker, eds., *The Journal of Esther Edwards Burr, 1754–1757*, Yale University Press, 1984. This is a series of letters written by Jonathan and Sarah Edwards' daughter, Esther Burr, to her friend Sally Prince between October 1754 and September 1757.

Melissa Kruger and Kirsten Wetherall, eds., *12 Faithful Women: Portraits of Steadfast Endurance*, Gospel Coalition, 2020. Includes a chapter by Courtney Reissig on Sarah Edwards.

George M. Marsden, *Jonathan Edwards: A Life*, Yale University Press, 2003. The most comprehensive biography to date, with access to the most recently available sources.

Kenneth P. Minkema and Harry S. Stout, 'The Edwardsean Tradition and the Antislavery Debate, 1740–1865', *The Journal of American History*, vol. 92, no. 1 (June 2005), pp. 47–74.

John Piper, 'How Could Jonathan Edwards Own Slaves? Wrestling with the History of a Hero', Desiring God, 10 August 2021, https://www.desiringgod.org/articles/how-could-jonathan-edwards-own-slaves.

John Piper and Justin Taylor, eds., *A God Entranced Vision of All Things: The Legacy of Jonathan Edwards*, Crossway, 2004. Includes a chapter by Noël Piper on Sarah Edwards, pp. 55–78.

Maggie Rowe, *An Uncommon Union: The Life and Love Of Sarah and Jonathan Edwards*, Vision Video, 2004. A film depicting Sarah's life and experience.

Thomas Sowell, 'The Real History of Slavery', *Black Rednecks and White Liberals*, Encounter Books, 2005, pp. 111–69.

Jonathan Edwards' works

Edward Hickman, ed. *The Works of Jonathan Edwards*, 2 volumes, Banner of Truth Trust, 1974.

Sereno Edwards Dwight, great-grandson of Jonathan and Sarah Edwards, compiled a 10-volume set of Edwards' writings – *The Works of President Edwards: With a Memoir of His Life,* 10 volumes, New York, 1830 – which Banner of Truth Trust reprinted in two volumes in 1974–75. That two-volume set begins with Dwight's *Memoir* of Jonathan Edwards, Edwards' farewell sermon to the Northampton church, some family trees and a list of Edwards' works.

The Works of Jonathan Edwards, 26 volumes, Yale University Press, 1977–2009, https://www.logos.com/product/15471/the-works-of-jonathan-edwards-yale-edition

Heaven: A World of Love, 1738, https://www.chapellibrary. org:8443/pdf/books/hawo.pdf. The final sermon in a series on 1 Corinthians 13.

Christ Exalted, or, Jesus Christ Gloriously Exalted Above All Evil in the Work of Redemption, 1738, https://www.biblebb.com/files/edwards/exalted.htm

Resolutions, 1722, https://www.chapellibrary.org/book/roje/resolutions-of-jonathan-edwards-the-edwardsjonathan

An Humble Attempt to Promote Explicit Agreement and Visible Union of God's People in Extraordinary Prayer, For the Revival of Religion and the Advancement of Christ's Kingdom on Earth, 1746 http://www.ccel.org/ccel/edwards/works2.viii.html

Further devotional resources

Nancy Leigh DeMoss, *Brokenness: The Heart God Revives*, Moody Publishers, 2008.

Erroll Hulse, *Let's Pray for Global Revival,* Chapel Library, 1998, https://www.chapellibrary.org/book/lpfg/lets-pray-for-global-revival-hulseerroll

Erroll Hulse, *Fellowship with the Triune God* (based on John Owen's *Union and Communion*), Fellowship with the Trinity, Chapel Library, 2009.

Donald S. Whitney, *Spiritual Disciplines for the Christian Life,* Nav Press, 2014.

Arthur Bennett, ed., *Valley of Vision: Puritan Prayers and Devotions,* Banner of Truth, 1975.

Operation World, book (7th edition, IVP, 2010) and other resources to help pray for the world, https://operationworld.org/

Acknowledgements

There has been a great increase of appreciation of the works of Jonathan Edwards over the past 70 years. I am thankful to God for the faith and courage of those who founded the Banner of Truth Trust in 1957. They led the way in a revival of interest in Edwards, and I want to pay special tribute to the work of Rev Iain Murray, who led that work for many years, and who has written extensively on Edwards. I also want to honour the work of John Piper and Desiring God Ministries in introducing the 'God Entranced Vision' of Jonathan Edwards to so many people in so many countries.

I owe a debt of gratitude to Dr Wayne Mack: as a young teenager I heard him preach on heaven and hell at the first Carey Family Conference in England. Those sermons inspired me to go on to read Jonathan Edwards' *Heaven: A World of Love*. That preaching, and that booklet, were formative influences in my conversion.

My late parents, Erroll and Lynette Hulse, were passionate about working for, and praying for, global evangelisation and revival. They set me an example of the importance of daily prayer for the nations, a vision promoted by Jonathan Edwards in his *Humble Attempt*.

I am deeply grateful to Professor Michael Haykin. He supervised my studies in church history at Toronto Baptist Seminary, and has encouraged me over the years to keep up my interest in church history. His own writings have been helpful to me, as to many others. I am grateful to him for his advice on this book. My thanks to Janice van Eck for her design work on *In Trouble and In Joy* back in 2003, and for her faithful friendship over many years. I am grateful to Graham Hind and Jonathan Pountney for their encouragement with this project. I would like to thank Mary Davis for her editorial work, and also Beth Lees and Sheri Newton at 10ofThose for their input. My thanks also goes to Jude May for her great work on the design.

I work as part of a team at The Christian Institute (christian. org.uk). I am grateful to God for the fellowship I enjoy with the team, and for the ministry of the Institute, which seeks to promote biblical truth and the glory of God in our nation and beyond. I am thankful to colleagues and friends who have read and commented on the book, including Janice van Eck, Sarah Aiken, Rachel Gillies, Julia Jones, Sally Gobbett, Elinor Magowan, Elisabeth Smyth and Willemien Gunnink. I'm especially grateful to Elinor Magowan for supplying some of the questions for reflection at the end of each chapter. The views expressed in this book are my own, as are any and all mistakes made.

I am grateful to Bishop Timothy Dudley-Smith for his wonderful renderings of so many Psalms and for permission to quote his version of Psalm 63.

Acknowledgements

My husband Bill is supportive of all my writing. More importantly, he daily points me to the boundless riches to be found in Christ.

Sharon James
London, 2022

Endnotes

1. Psalm 63, as rendered by Timothy Dudley-Smith in the hymn, 'God is My Great Desire', tune: Leoni, in *Praise!* 63, Praise Trust, 2000. Copyright: author/Oxford University Press.

Introduction

1. Edward Hickman, ed. *The Works of Jonathan Edwards*, 2 volumes, Banner of Truth Trust, 1974, vol. 1, p. l.
2. John Piper, 'How Could Jonathan Edwards Own Slaves? Wrestling with the History of a Hero', *Desiring God,* 10 August 2021, https://www.desiringgod.org/articles/how-could-jonathan-edwards-own-slaves (accessed 17 August 2021).
3. Jonathan Edwards, *Heaven: A World of Love,* Banner of Truth Trust, 2008.
4. The account of Sarah's life is substantially the same as the biographical sketch in Sharon James, *In Trouble and In Joy,* Evangelical Press, 2003.

Chapter 1

1. William Bradford, *Of Plymouth Plantation,* Dover Publications, 2006. This is a republication of Bradford's *History of the Plymouth Settlement,* 1608–1650, first published in 1920.

2. George M. Marsden, *Jonathan Edwards: A Life*, Yale University Press, p. 15. Rev Williams and two of the children were released in 1706. Eunice, age seven at the time of the attack, was kept captive. She converted to Catholicism, and later married an Indian. Marsden, *Jonathan Edwards*, p. 219.

3. Indentured servants, including many from Europe, were widely used.

4. Jonathan and Sarah owned slaves. By the standards of their day, this was not surprising. Yet, there were some, notably the Quakers and even more importantly, Puritan leaders like Samuel Sewall (1652–1730), who condemned both the slave trade and slavery. See Samuel Sewall, *The Selling of Joseph* (Bartholomew Green and John Allen, 1700); Susan Stinson, 'The Other Side of the Paper: Jonathan Edwards as Slave-Owner', *Valley Advocate*, 5 April, 2012, https://valleyadvocate.com/2012/04/05/the-other-side-of-the-paper-jonathan-edwards-as-slave-owner/ (accessed 1 July 2021); Marsden, *Jonathan Edwards*, p. 20. For a wider context on the history of slavery in North America, see Thomas Sowell, 'The Real History of Slavery', *Black Rednecks and White Liberals*, Encounter Books, 2005, pp. 111–69.

5. Note on Job 31:15 written in the early 1730s. Cited by Piper, 'How Could Jonathan Edwards Own Slaves?'

Chapter 2

1. Edward Hickman, ed. *The Works of Jonathan Edwards*, 2 volumes, Banner of Truth Trust, 1974, vol. 1, p. xxxix.

2. Hickman, ed., *Works*, vol. 1, pp. xxxix–xl.

3. As late as 1880, the age of consent stood at 10 or 12 in many American states. It was raised across the United States by the

early twentieth century. During the eighteenth century it was common for women to marry at a young age.

4. Marsden, *Jonathan Edwards*, pp. 143–45.

5. 'Christ's offices': he is for his people our prophet, priest and king. We need him in these roles because we are ignorant of God (in need of a prophet), guilty (in need of a priest) and helpless (in need of a king).

6. Michael A. G. Haykin, 'Nearness to Christ as the Creature's Greatest Happiness: Extracts from the Diary of Sarah Edwards', *Banner of Truth Magazine*, June 2014, pp. 21–23, https://banneroftruth.org/uk/store/magazine/june-2014/; also in Michael A. G. Haykin, *Eight Women of Faith*, Crossway, 2016, pp. 70–72.

Chapter 3

1. Hickman, ed., *Works*, vol. 1, p. cxxxii.

2. Hickman, ed., *Works*, vol. 2, p. 244.

3. Hickman, ed., *Works*, vol. 1, p. xiv.

4. Hickman, ed., *Works*, vol. 1, pp. xx–xxii.

5. Hickman, ed., *Works*, vol. 1, p. xlviii.

6. Hickman, ed., *Works*, vol. 1, pp. xlvi–xlvii.

7. Hickman, ed., *Works*, vol. 1, p. xiv.

Chapter 4

1. Hickman, ed., *Works*, vol. 1, pp. xl–xli.

2. Hickman, ed., *Works*, vol. 1, p. xlv.

3. Iain H. Murray, *Jonathan Edwards: A New Biography*, Banner of Truth Trust, 1987, pp. 9, 14.

4. Murray, *Jonathan Edwards*, p. 187.

5. Hickman, ed., *Works*, vol. 1, p. 376. During the eighteenth

and nineteenth centuries, a catch-all description for female mental/physical/hormonal illnesses was the 'vapours'.

6. Hickman, ed., *Works*, vol. 1, p. 376.

7. Aaron Burr Jr was Vice President during President Thomas Jefferson's first term as President from 1801 to 1805. He was the son of Jonathan and Sarah's daughter, Esther, and her husband Aaron Burr. Meteorically successful in terms of position achieved, he was a disaster in emotional and moral terms. He was an exception – the vast majority of Jonathan and Sarah's descendants followed their example of integrity and service.

8. A. E. Winship, quoted in Elisabeth D. Dodds, *Marriage to a Difficult Man: The 'Uncommon Union' of Jonathan and Sarah Edwards,* Westminster Press, 1975, p. 38.

Chapter 5

1. Hickman, ed., *Works*, vol. 1, p. xlvi.

2. Jonathan Edwards, 'Christian Charity, or the Duty of Charity to the Poor Explained and Enforced' in Hickman, ed., *Works,* vol. 2, pp. 163–73; Sharon James, 'Compassion and Wisdom: The Response of Jonathan Edwards to the Problem of Poverty', *Baptist Review of Theology*, vol. 5, no. 1, Spring 1995, https://www.biblicalstudies.org.uk/pdf/brt/05–1_053.pdf (accessed 12 July 2021).

3. We noted in Chapter 3 that the minister's wife usually sat in a seat next to the pulpit facing the congregation.

4. Hickman, ed., *Works,* vol. 1, p. xlii.

5. Marsden, *Jonathan Edwards*, p. 154. 'Frothy' in conversation, ie superficial and shallow.

6. Jonathan Edwards, 'A Faithful Narrative of the Surprising

Work of God in the Conversion of Many Hundred Souls in Northampton', 1737, in Hickman, ed., *Works*, vol. 1, p. 348.

7. Marsden, *Jonathan Edwards*, p. 205.

8. Murray, *Jonathan Edwards*, pp. 163–64.

9. Marsden, *Jonathan Edwards*, p. 207.

10. Marsden, *Jonathan Edwards*, p. 214. The eldest daughter had shown signs of salvation some years before.

11. Hickman, ed., *Works*, vol. 1, p. lxviii.

Chapter 6

1. Hickman, ed., *Works*, vol. 1, pp. 366–430.

2. Hickman, ed., *Works*, vol. 1, p. 376.

3. In the next century, long after their deaths, Jonathan and Sarah Edwards' great-grandson, Sereno Edwards Dwight, published *The Works of President Edwards* (10 volumes, New York, 1830). He included a 'Memoir' of Jonathan Edwards, which incorporated Sarah's account of her revival experience, this time attributed to her, and in the first person. This chapter contains this account, as given by Sereno Edwards Dwight. Chapter XI of 'Memoirs of Jonathan Edwards' in Hickman, ed, *Works*, vol. 1, pp. lxii-lxx.

4. Ralph Erskine (1685–1752), *Gospel Sonnets: The Believer's Principles Concerning Faith and Sense*, New York, 1859, p. 523.

5. 'Munition', ie fortification, place of defence well supplied with ammunition.

6. Isaac Watts (1674–1748), English author, hymn writer and theologian.

7. 'Complacential': a peaceful satisfaction (in God).

8. 'Avocations', ie tasks.

9. Probably Isaac Watts, 'O, the delights, the heavenly joys, The

glories of the place', 1707, https://hymnary.org/text/o_the_delights_the_heavenly_joys (accessed 12 July 2021).

10. 'Elysium', ie paradise.

11. God's presence went 'with' the ark of the covenant (Exodus 25:22; 2 Samuel 6:12). Sarah is alluding to the 'ark' as a symbol of the presence of God's glory.

12. 'The Penitential Cries' in John Mason and Thomas Shepard, *Thirty-Two Hymns,* 1693, https://quod.lib.umich.edu/e/eebo/A54092.0001.001?view=toc (accessed 4 March 2022).

13. An allusion to the clusters of grapes gathered by the spies who went in to the 'earthly' Canaan (Numbers 13:23–24) before the conquest.

14. 'Alacrity', ie cheerful willingness.

15. Mason and Shepard, 'The Penitential Cries'.

16. Elizabeth Singer Rowe (1674–1737), English author, poet and hymn writer. Her book *Devout Exercises of the Heart* was published after her death with a preface by Isaac Watts.

17. Hickman, ed., *Works,* vol. 1, p. lxviii. Iain Murray comments that many modern writers have been nonplussed by Sarah Edwards' experience, putting it down to nervous instability or pathological traits: Murray, *Jonathan Edwards,* p. 196. But believers who delight in God more than anything else have been condemned as 'fanatical' or 'enthusiasts' in every age: 'The natural person does not accept the things of the Spirit of God, for they are folly to him, and he is not able to understand them because they are spiritually discerned' (1 Corinthians 2:14).

18. Hickman, ed., *Works,* vol. 1, p. lxix.

19. Hickman, ed., *Works,* vol. 1, p. lxix.

20. 'Distemper', ie derangement, a mental and physical disorder.

21. Hickman, ed., *Works,* vol. 1, p. lxix.

22. Hickman, ed., *Works*, vol. 1, p. 390.

23. Jonathan Edwards wrote that one reason for the decline of revival was that 'physical excitement had been greater than the human constitution can, for a long period, endure. Nothing, it should be remembered, exhausts the strength and animal spirits like feeling. One hour of intense joy or intense sorrow will more entirely prostrate the frame than weeks of close study.' Hickman, ed., *Works,* vol. 1, p. xliv.

24. 'Still the small inward voice I hear | That whispers all my sins forgiven | Still the atoning blood is near | That quenched the flaming wrath of heaven | *I feel* the life his wounds impart | *I feel* my Saviour in my heart.' Original verse 5 of 'And Can It Be' by Charles Wesley, 1783, emphasis mine.

Chapter 7

1. Marsden, *Jonathan Edwards*, pp. 247–48. Eunice was born in May 1743.

2. Marsden, *Jonathan Edwards*, p. 317.

3. The many atrocities committed against Protestant believers in France during the fifteenth century and sixteenth century were well known. See 'The Huguenots: Evangelicals Persecuted by the French State', The Christian Institute, https://www.christian.org.uk/wp-content/uploads/huguenots.pdf (accessed 7 April 2022).

4. At this time, before medical care was provided in hospitals, female relatives and friends were usually called on to nurse the sick and dying; Sarah's ready response to this request for help would not have seemed unusual.

5. Solomon Stoddard believed that he had experienced conversion after he was ordained to the ministry and *while*

he was administering the Lord's Supper. (It is possible that he gained clear assurance for the first time.) After that he always maintained that partaking of the Lord's Supper could be used as a means of grace, even a means of saving grace. Murray, *Jonathan Edwards*, p. 79.

6. Quoted in Murray, *Jonathan Edwards*, pp. 485–87.

7. Edwards, 'Farewell Sermon' in Hickman, ed., *Works*, vol. 1, p. cciv.

8. Marsden, *Jonathan Edwards*, p. 327.

9. Carol F. Karlsen and Laurie Crumpacker, eds, *The Journal of Esther Edwards Burr, 1754–57*, Yale University Press, 1984, p. 54.

10. Mahican Indians, otherwise known as Mohican, Muhhakaneok, Stockbridge or Housatonic. Marsden, *Jonathan Edwards*, p. 375.

11. Marsden, *Jonathan Edwards*, p. 383.

12. Murray, *Jonathan Edwards*, p. 379.

13. Marsden, *Jonathan Edwards*, p. 391.

14. Marsden, *Jonathan Edwards*, p. 387.

Chapter 8

1. Esther was able to find strong consolation in God, writing to her parents: 'He has, in an uncommon degree, discovered Himself to be an all-sufficient God, a full fountain of all good. Although all streams were cut off, yet the fountain is left full. I think I have been enabled to cast my care upon Him and have found great peace and calmness in my mind, such as this world cannot give nor take. I have had uncommon freedom and nearness to the throne of grace. God has seemed sensibly near in such a supporting and comfortable manner that I think I have never experienced the like.' Hickman, ed., *Works*, vol. 1, p. clxxiii.

2. The college had moved location by December 1756.
3. Murray, *Jonathan Edwards*, p. 10.
4. Inducing a mild dose of smallpox to produce immunity.
5. Hickman, ed. *Works*, vol. 1, p. clxxviii.
6. Hickman, ed., *Works*, vol. 1, p. clxxix.
7. Hickman, ed., *Works*, vol. 1, p. clxxix.
8. Hickman, ed., *Works*, vol. 1, p. clxxx. Elizabeth, the Edwards' youngest daughter, died aged 14 soon after her parents. The other younger Edwards children, along with Esther's two infants, would be cared for by the older Edwards daughters and their husbands. The surviving four Edwards daughters – Sarah, Mary, Lucy and Eunice – all married (between them they bore 36 children, some of whom died in infancy). Timothy, Jonathan and Pierpont each became eminent in public life; each of them married (and between them they bore 29 children, some of whom died in infancy).

Chapter 9

1. Jonathan Edwards, 'Christ Exalted or Jesus Christ Gloriously Exalted Above All Evil in the Work of Redemption', a sermon preached in 1738 from 1 Corinthians 15:25–26, https://www.biblebb.com/files/edwards/exalted.htm (accessed 12 July 2021).
2. Later published as a book: *The History of Redemption: Theological Writings of Jonathan Edwards (1703–58)*, https://www.apuritansmind.com/puritan-favorites/jonathan-edwards/theological/the-history-of-redemption-by-jonathan-edwards/ (accessed 8 May 2022).
3. Nehemiah Strong, who would later go on to become a professor of mathematics and natural philosophy at Yale.

4. Marsden, *Jonathan Edwards*, p. 195. The sermon series formed the basis of Edwards, *A History of the Work of Redemption*, 1739, https://www.monergism.com/history-work-redemption-ebook (accessed 12 July 2021); http://www.preachershelp.net/wp-content/uploads/2014/11/redemption-edwards-481.pdf (accessed 12 July 2021).

5. These are George Marsden's words relating to Edwards' theology in Marsden, *Jonathan Edwards*, p. 488.

6. Daniel 2:35, 'Then the iron, the clay, the bronze, the silver, and the gold, all together were broken in pieces, and became like the chaff of the summer threshing floors; and the wind carried them away, so that not a trace of them could be found. But the stone that struck the image became a great mountain and filled the whole earth.' Jonathan Edwards was confident that Christ's kingdom, from small beginnings, would ultimately fill the whole earth. Marsden, *Jonathan Edwards*, p. 488; Stephen J. Nichols, *A Time for Confidence*, Reformation Trust, 2016, pp. 112–116.

7. See chapter 6.

8. Murray, *Jonathan Edwards*, p. xxxi.

9. George Herbert, *The Temper I*, 1633, https://www.poetryfoundation.org/poems/44374/the-temper-i (accessed 4 March 2022). George Herbert (1593–1633) was an English metaphysical poet, and minister in the Church of England. 'Temper' in the title alludes to a proportion between qualities.

10. Jonathan Edwards, *An Humble Attempt*, 1746, http://www.ccel.org/ccel/edwards/works2.viii.html (accessed 12 July 2021). A challenge to God's people to unite in prayer for the evangelisation of the world.

Endnotes

11. Dan Graves, 'August Francke, Unto Us a Son Is Given – 1601–1700', Church History timelines, christianity.com (accessed 10 August 2022).

About the Author

SHARON JAMES is an author, conference speaker and Social Policy Analyst for The Christian Institute. She has degrees in history (Cambridge University) and theology (M.Div., Toronto Baptist Seminary), and a doctorate from the University of Wales. She is married to Bill, who is Principal of London Seminary. They have two grown up children and six grandchildren.

Her books include: *Ann Judson: A Missionary Life for Burma; God's Design for Women in an Age of Gender Confusion; How Christianity Transformed the World; The Lies We are Told, the Truth We Must Hold;* and *Gender Ideology: What Do Christians Need to Know?* For more information about Sharon James's work visit sharonjames.org.